Great Montana
BEAR STORIES

Great Montana
BEAR
STORIES

BEN LONG

RIVERBEND PUBLISHING

RIVERBEND PUBLISHING
P.O. Box 5833
Helena, MT 59604
1-866-RVR-BEND (787-2363)
www.riverbendpublishing.com

For Karen, my favorite camping partner.
Sleep tight; it's probably just the wind...

Acknowledgments

I HAD THE PLEASURE OF DIGGING THROUGH DECADES OF MONTANA'S newspaper archives, from both modern and historic times. These included Kalispell's Daily Inter Lake and Weekly News; the Hungry Horse News of Columbia Falls, the Great Falls Tribune, the Missoula Missoulian; and the Bozeman Daily Chronicle. I owe a debt to the many hardworking newspaper journalists who first reported on many of these stories, under the crunch of deadlines.

Foremost, I appreciate the many people who made time in their busy schedules to talk to me and tell me their bear stories. Especially, I am grateful to the family of Timothy "Omar" Hilston, of Great Falls, for talking to me while still feeling the raw pain of the loss of their family member. At Montana Department of Fish, Wildlife and Parks, I thank Keith Aune, Jamie Jonkel, Rick Mace, Mike Madel, Tim Thier and Eric Wenum. At the National Park Service, I thank Steve Frye, Steve Gniadek, Charlie Logan, and Amy Vanderbilt and retired ranger Bert Gildart. At the U.S. Fish and Wildlife Service, I'm grateful to Wayne Kasworm. Thanks go to retired Montana game wardens Lou Kis and Dave Wedum and also to Carrie Hunt, the driving force behind the Wind River Bear Dog Institute and savior of many a grizzly bear. A grateful tip of the coffee mug to G. George Ostrom, the unstoppable newspaperman and radio broadcaster from KOFI in Kalispell. Thanks also to Brian Peck, who works to conserve grizzly bears and their habitat from Columbia Falls. Kerrie Byrne, Karen Nichols and Gen Long looked over the copy, along with the good folks at Riverbend Publishing. Thanks to Chris Cauble, for dreaming up this wonderful idea of a book.

Contents

Preface: Entering the Den of the Cave Bear

THE OLDEST ART GALLERY IN THE WORLD IS IN THE ARDECHE RIVER Valley near Avignon, France. It's no place for claustrophobes. To enter one must squeeze through a narrow gap in a limestone cliff and into the dungeon-dark Chauvet Cave. Only very rare visitors delve into the catacombs, ducking the stalactites and squeezing through interior chambers. If you shine a flashlight on the walls, animals from a forgotten world stare back: shaggy rhinos, woolly mammoths, cave lions, northern leopards, and surreal creatures that are part human and part beast. People painted these images roughly 35,000 years ago. One painting stands out, bold and simple in great strokes of ochre and charcoal. You would recognize it instantly. It's a bear.

Specifically, it's a cave bear, *Ursus spelaeus*, a hulking species that disappeared at the end of the Pleistocene Ice Age about 20,000 years ago. The cave bear lived alongside ancient Asians and Europeans. Modern explorers found 147 cave bear skulls in the Chauvet Cave—including one skull placed on a slab of rock like an offering on an altar. So keep this in mind: This book is part of a tradition that stretches back more than 350 centuries—the tradition of telling bear stories.

When the Ice Age glaciers melted from the Rocky Mountains, they left Montana a vast and wild stage where people and bears shared top billing. At least 11,000 years ago, the mysterious Clovis people roamed Montana, hunting mammoths and bison and living among bears. They left behind large, distinctive spear points along the Belly River and the Shields Valley. We can only imagine what bear stories the Clovis told in the shadows of their fires.

The ancestors of the Blackfeet, Crow, Kootenai, and other tribes roamed the tundra-like alpine of the Beartooth Plateau, the cedar forests of the Yaak River, the windswept bluffs of the Ekalaka Hills, and the bison prairies of Medicine Lake. The bears roamed all those places as well. The balance of power between people and bears was subtle and ancient. Respect flowed both directions. Native Americans and bears shared food from wild parsnip to huckleberries to bison, so diplomacy was essential. The Kootenai conducted elaborate ceremonies to safeguard themselves from bear attacks. The Blackfeet called the grizzly the "real bear," just as they called the sacred bison meat the "real meat."

On April 29, 1805, Lewis and Clark shattered these age-old patterns in a volley of gunfire. Meriwether Lewis killed the first grizzly bear of that famous expedition at Big Muddy Creek in what is today far northeastern Montana. Clark followed with a second grizzly a few days later. The explorers knew of black bears from Virginia and Kentucky, but they had never seen a predator as large, tough, and prone to fighting back as a grizzly. Grizzlies gave the explorers fits, particularly around Great Falls. For the rest of their trek, the explorers killed grizzlies at nearly every opportunity. This set the precedent for the next 200 years.

This book focuses on bear stories of this modern period, starting around 1830. In the two centuries after the Corps of Discovery, a long string of prospectors, mountain men, pioneers, and cowboys all told bear stories. Some of Charlie Russell's most dynamic oil paintings tell bear stories, depicting true tales of buckaroos capturing a grizzly with lariats or a marksman saving the bacon of a hapless hunter. The first man to photograph grizzly bears in the wild—a hunter named William Wright—lived in Missoula and hunted in the Bitterroots.

For many Americans today, simply seeing a wild bear—any bear—is a once-in-a-lifetime adventure. Every summer Montana hosts millions of visitors who spend a fortune on Teddy bears, bear T-shirts, coffee mugs, and even bear-paw salad tongs. Each summer, visitors send postcards home with their own bear stories scribbled on the back. Those of us who live in Montana tell and re-tell our own bear stories until the stories are as polished as river stones.

Bears seize our imaginations quite unlike any other animal. Bears are beautiful animals, but so are gazelles, dolphins, and rainbow trout. Our minds blow bears far out of proportion. We can't seem to help it. Outdoor magazines are read by millions of people in the United States and Canada, few of whom will ever see a grizzly bear outside of a zoo. Yet every outdoor magazine regularly presents grizzlies on its cover, usually nose-to-the-camera, baring its fangs. (Here's a trade secret: The bear isn't really roaring. It's a trained animal model performing for a marshmallow treat.) Editors know bears sell magazines.

Why are we so fascinated by bears? In *The Sacred Paw*, anthropologist Paul Shepherd wrote of prehistoric humans' fascination with bears. "When a man looked into the eyes of a cave bear, he received a deep impression of manlike consciousness." Look at any number of Far Side cartoons featuring bears; it doesn't take much imagination to give a bear human characteristics or motivations. Bears and humans have much in common. Bears occasionally stand on their hind legs. Bears also walk on flat feet that look a bit like ours. It's a cliché of bear books to report that the musculature of a skinned bear looks startlingly human.

Bears, like humans, are omnivorous. They enjoy a fresh salad but crave a good, rare steak. Bears are intelligent enough to learn from their successes and mistakes. Mother bears, like mother humans, invest great quantities of time and energy raising their young, teaching them to make a living and get along with others. Bears are highly individualistic. While it may be overstating facts to say each bear has a personality, each bear certainly has an individual temperament and individual likes and dislikes.

But there is another power driving our bear stories. That is fear. Today, only a microscopic percentage of human beings are ever at risk of being eaten by a wild animal, but this was not always the case. For most of five million years of hominid history, our ancestors were hunted by lions, leopards, and assorted other large carnivores. Our careless and foolish ancestors were picked off and removed from the gene pool. This left its impression on our DNA. We are genetically hard-wired to fear big predators. Even in the modern world, the idea of being captured, dismembered, and actually eaten by something triggers a very special sort of dread. This is not something we can shake off lightly.

Fear kept our ancestors alive, but fear can also delude us. Statistically speaking, bears are not particularly dangerous. In Europe, Asia, and North America, brown bears (or what we call grizzlies) kill about five people annually, worldwide. Black bears live only in North America and kill about five people annually in the United States and Canada. Disease-carrying mosquitoes, on the other hand, kill millions of people around the world every year. The American Automobile Association figures deer contribute to the deaths of 120 Americans annually by their habit of dashing in front of speeding vehicles. But who wants to believe that mosquitoes and deer are more dangerous than bears?

In Montana, fewer than 15 people have died in bear attacks in 100 years of statehood. Meanwhile, in any one year more than 250 people die violent, bloody deaths in Montana highway accidents. On average, about 33 Montanans are murdered annually.

The fact is, visitors in Glacier National Park are far more likely to drown, be struck by a falling rock, fall over a cliff, or tumble down a waterfall than be killed by a bear. The fact is, as many tourists in Yellowstone National Park have been killed by falling lodgepole pine trees or fatally struck by lightning as have been killed by bears. The fact is, avalanches in 2001 and 2002 killed more people in Montana than bears have killed in the state's history. But facts pale compared to instinctive fear.

If fear is a survival tool, so is the story. Useful stories help us live long, healthy, productive lives. One purpose of this book is to help people survive. All of us who enjoy wild country can learn from mistakes made by our fellows. The regulations, folk wisdom, and woodcraft we follow in bear country are simply lessons learned from a school of very hard knocks. It's not that the wilderness is particularly dangerous compared to the city. Rather, the hazards one might face in the wilds are different than those we face in civilization. We are an increasingly urban people, but we still need stories of the wilderness.

But another kind of survival is at stake here besides the survival of individual readers. That is the survival of bears themselves. Of the eight species of bears in the world, only the American black bear, *Ursus americanus,* has not been threatened or endangered with extinction. Yet even the black bear is in trouble or has been eliminated in 17 of the 49 United States in which it was native. The grizzly bear, *Ursus arctos,* is a threatened species in the lower forty-eight states under the Endangered Species Act. Montana, with its estimated 800 to 1,000 grizzly bears, represents the grizzly's last, best toehold south of Canada.

In Montana, we are conserving grizzly bears not only for the rest of the country, but also for our children's children. Bears are running out of room. As Missoula biologist John Weaver once said, "Space is the air of the great beasts who roam the earth. Now is their final breath."

I hope that by telling these stories, by examining the occasional violence between bears and people, we can learn something about sharing Montana with our greatest neighbors. If we do this, and if we protect adequate wild space, we can continue to tell stories about the "real bears," and not simply recall the bones of extinct creatures and old paintings on cave walls.

Joe Meek, Mountain Man

WHEN EXPLORERS AND TRAPPERS ENTERED MONTANA IN THE EARLY 1800s, it was as if they cracked the lid on a giant treasure chest. Explorers were astounded by the vast numbers of bison, elk, and beaver and could only imagine the wealth in silver, gold, and timber to be exploited by generations to come. In those early decades, beaver pelts were simply a valuable natural resource similar to oil or diamonds today. The race to collect pelts was fast and furious. The fur trade introduced some of the most colorful characters in American history: mountain men like Jim Bridger, Jedediah Smith, and Kit Carson.

One less famous but equally colorful character was Joseph L. Meek, fellow traveler of Bridger, Smith, and Carson. Starting in the 1830s—the heart of the mountain man era—Meek spent eleven years roaming the Rocky Mountain West before settling in Oregon. He was a trapper, warrior, and lawman. One could describe Joe Meek with a hundred adjectives, but "meek," is not on the list.

Meek was born in Virginia in 1810, four years after Lewis and Clark returned from their epic trek to the Pacific Ocean. Like Lewis and Clark, Meek's parents were Virginia blueblood elite. But young Joe preferred to loiter around the slave quarters than attend school. When a teacher pressed the matter,

Joe retaliated with his fists. In 1828 at age 18, Meek left Virginia. He figured his parents just uttered *good riddance.* A year later Meek was in St. Louis, the raw edge of the American frontier. He wished to go as far from the stifling heat and society of Virginia as a young man could reach. Meek signed on with the Rocky Mountain Fur Company, which had designs on the beaver streams of Montana.

Examining a later portrait of Meek, it's clear he was proud to be a mountain man. He posed with a stout jaw, a high chin, and eyes that stare at the photographer as if the fellow owed him a large sum of money. The portrait captures him wearing a jaunty fox-skin cap and fringed leather jacket, leaning on the muzzle of a rifle. He stands before a painted backdrop of a mountain scene.

The standard mountain man clichés apply to Meek. He wore buckskins and a beard. He carried a rifle, traps, and great bundles of pelts aboard mules. He married a Nez Perce woman he re-named Virginia. Sitting around the campfire, Meek could tell tales with the best of them. His remarkable stories might have been lost had they not been written down by an adoring biographer in the book *River of the West,* published in 1870, five years before Meek died. His stories paint a picture of Montana in the 1830s when, as Charlie Russell said, "the land belonged to God."

●　●　●

COMPETITION IN THE FUR TRADE was international and sometimes literally cutthroat. Empires like Rocky Mountain Fur Company and the Hudson's Bay Company waged commercial war. Their tactic was to sweep entire river drainages, wiping out the beavers before competitors arrived. Local Indian tribes were embroiled in these rivalries as allies with certain fur companies, enemies of others. These turf battles were often quite bloody for humans, to say nothing of the beavers. Trappers faced blizzards, blistering deserts, and swift, frigid rivers. The job's fringe benefits included lots of fresh air, plenty of adventure, and the fact that the boss, the law, and the clergy were thousands of miles away. As if the rugged wilderness, international intrigue, and guerrilla warfare weren't enough, mountain men also had to contend with grizzly bears.

The Yellowstone River runs the length of Montana like the state's femoral artery. When Capt. William Clark descended the Yellowstone in 1806, he was flabbergasted over the enormous herds of bison and elk he passed daily. At one point, Clark wrote in his journal that he would no longer mention the abundance of wildlife along the Yellowstone, since no one was likely to believe him anyway. By 1830, the river still teemed with wildlife, potential wealth, and adventure. There was no place Joe Meek would rather be.

While the real money was in beaver furs, the Rocky Mountain Fur Company also paid four dollars for every grizzly pelt that made its way to St. Louis. With this incentive mountain men killed hundreds of grizzly bears. Such a tally is doubly remarkable given the weaponry of the mountain men. They were hardly "loaded for bear." Meek probably carried a Hawken plains rifle, which blew a half-inch ball to its target but had limited range and penetration. Moreover, the gun fired only once. To reload, Meek had to measure a charge of gunpowder, pour it down the muzzle, and ram the wadding and ball down the muzzle with a long stick. The Hawken featured important technological advances over the flintlocks carried by Lewis and Clark but was still pathetically under powered for dangerous animals.

In 1836 Meek roamed the Cross Creeks region of the Yellowstone. He shared his duties with two partners, a fellow named Mark Head and another man identified only as Gardiner.

While searching for beaver one day, the trappers watched an adult grizzly digging roots in the creek bottom. The bear's long, curving claws turned the sod over while it nipped the exposed roots with its incisors. Noting the hungry bear was feeding intently, Meek dismounted, handed his mule's reins to his fellow trappers, and put on a stalk.

Meek moved in slowly, keeping the wind to his face and hiding behind the cover of the streamside willows. Gradually Meek crept toward the bear. His moccasins took him silently within forty yards. When Meek was so close he figured he could not miss, he shouldered his rifle, took aim, and squeezed the trigger.

The Hawken rifle was ignited by a percussion cap—a small blasting cap that sparks the charge of gunpowder when the hammer falls. These caps were moody and easily ruined by moisture. When Meek pulled the trigger, he expected a boom. Instead, Joe just heard the "pop" of the falling hammer. The rifle did not fire. The bear heard the pop, too. And charged.

Meek turned and ran but soon found himself cornered against a stone outcrop. As he scrambled to replace the rifle's faulty percussion cap, the bear tore at him. Her claws caught the heavy, hooded garment called a "capote" which Meek had belted around his waist. Desperate and terrified, Meek stuffed the muzzle of his rifle down the bear's throat. The rifle had two triggers, one to "set" the hair-trigger and the hair-trigger that fired the gun. Flustered by his circumstances, Meek fumbled with the triggers.

The bear slapped the gun barrel out of its mouth just as Meek finally fired. The shot enveloped both man and bear in a cloud of black-powder smoke, but it simply wounded and confused the bear, making it more furious.

Just then, Meek noticed a second bear. A cub rushed in as if to assist its mother at disemboweling this bearded intruder.

The female briefly turned her attention from Meek to the cub. In the words of Meek's biographer, the bear began "boxing it about in a most unmotherly fashion."

While the female was distracted, Meek drew his knife and made to stab the bear behind the ear. Meek wasn't packing any Boy Scout pocketknife, rather a remodeled butcher knife called a "scalper." As Joe prepared to strike, the bear knocked the knife from Meek's hand, "nearly severing his forefinger."

Trapper Joe seemed doomed to a painful death. But then another cub rushed in. Again the female left Meek to cuff the second cub. Seizing another opportunity, Joe drew his tomahawk, took aim on the bear's broad skull and bashed her a good one. The bear collapsed at Joe's feet, her skull fatally cleft.

What became of the cubs, we do not know. According to Meek's biographer, the bear was skinned and stuffed in a diorama at a St. Louis wax museum. There, Joe was rendered in life-size wax, his fateful hatchet blow frozen for years to come. If there had been one, Joe Meek would have been on his way to the Mountain Man Hall of Fame.

But he wasn't done with the bears quite yet.

*   *   *

IN THE AUTUMN OF 1830, Meek trapped along Rosebud Creek, south of today's Forsyth. Again, Meek was working with two companions. They happened across an autumn-fat cow bison and killed her for supper. As snow fell that evening, the trio made camp in a stand of aspen trees. The men feasted on fresh bison and slept heavily on full stomachs. According to the biography, Meek and the men crawled into their bedrolls and used the choice cuts of bison beef as pillows. This, Meek said, was "hunter fashion."

It's no surprise that a pile of raw meat might attract a varmint or two. Such trouble is even more likely in autumn, when animals are desperate to put on weight for the winter. No matter. Meek's squad slept soundly atop their meat pillows while snow covered their sleeping bodies. Gradually, the night paled toward dawn.

Meek awoke "to something very large and heavy walking over him and snuffling about him with the most insulting freedom." Meek opened an eye to see a grizzly standing on top of him. Meek lay perfectly still as the bear sniffed around, just inches from Meek's face. The bear's teeth then snatched the prime cut of bison meat stashed under Meek's head and it lumbered off to eat.

The visitor woke Meek's companions. When the bear returned for a second helping, Meek's fellow trappers moved to shoot the animal.

"No, no," cautioned Meek. "Hold on, or the brute will kill us for sure."

So the men pulled the covers over their heads, peeking out as they dared. The bear continued to "promenade" over the bedrolls, sniffing out a second helping of bison. "However," Meek said, "he couldn't quite make out our style, and finally took fright, and ran down the mountain."

"Wanting to be revenged for his impudence, I went after him," Meek said. "Seeing a good chance, I shot him dead. Then I took my turn at running over him awhile!"

Mountain men were long on bravado but sometimes dreadfully short of common sense. Today, almost any city slicker on a backpacking vacation in Montana knows to string his food ten feet up in a tree and well away from the tent. Evidently, mountain men like Joe Meek had to learn this lesson the hard way.

• • •

MEEK DIDN'T ALWAYS GET THE LAST LAUGH. Another season along the Yellowstone, Meek hunted with a trapper named Hawkins.

Together they spied a large, lone grizzly on the opposite bank. They tethered their mules, checked their rifles, and stalked about a mile until they were directly across the river from the bear. As a team, Meek and Hawkins drew, aimed, and fired. The guns exploded in sparks and smoke. The bear fell over with a thud.

Figuring the bear was dead for certain, the two hunters prepared to cross the river and skin their prize. Buckskin clothing shrinks and stiffens when wet, so the men stripped naked except for their belts and skinning knives and swam the river.

When Meek and Hawkins reached the far shore, they found the bear very much alive. Indeed, the bear recovered swiftly and charged after the two men. Meek and Hawkins launched themselves over the bank and into the river. The bear tumbled after them. Hawkins swam downstream while Meek fought his way up-river. Eventually the bear lost energy or interest. Hawkins and Meek pulled themselves ashore and regrouped.

"And then we traveled back a mile and more to where our mules were left," Meek recalled, "a bear on one side of the river and *two bares* on the other."

* * *

MUCH HAS BEEN SPECULATED about the "original" character of the grizzly bear, before men with rifles persecuted the animal. The question is, are today's grizzlies less bold and aggressive than the bears met by the mountain men? Some experts speculate that the most aggressive bears were killed off, leaving more timid bears to reproduce.

The journals of mountain men are saturated with gory clashes with grizzly bears. These might lead one to believe that the historic race of grizzlies was more cantankerous than the modern breed. Meriwether Lewis believed that the Great Plains grizzly's diet of bison meat made it more ferocious than the grizzlies in Idaho's Bitterroot Mountains that subsisted mostly on roots, berries and fish.

In his book, *Mountain Men and the Grizzly,* Fred R. Gowans collected about a hundred mountain man journal entries regarding grizzly bears, most of them violent. Of those violent, most occurred after the hunter stalked a grizzly bear and then annoyed it with a puny muzzleloader. Not uncommonly, wounded bears killed or severely mauled the mountain men. Explorers from Lewis and Clark on down wrote of grizzly bears as horrible monsters that would rather kill a man than run from him. These early descriptions earned the grizzly bear its first scientific name, *Ursus horribilis.* (Later, that name was modified to *Ursus arctos.* The Montana subspecies is still called *Ursus arctos horribilis.*)

But if grizzlies really were the vicious, man-eating monsters those early American explorers described, Indians never would have survived in North America for tens of thousands of years. While historians often retold the stories of bears attacking mountain men, they disregarded the bears that fled mountain men at the first whiff of them. In his book, *Lewis and Clark, Pioneering Naturalists,* historian Paul R. Cutright put it well: Mountain men like Meek or explorers like Lewis and Clark "gained most of their information about the disposition of the grizzly bear while looking down the barrels of their Kentucky rifles. They saw only wounded animals, maddened with pain and fear."

Exaggerated as they may have been, the mountain men's descriptions of the grizzly bear burned like a brand into the American imagination. In the 200 years since, bears are still trying to live down this reputation.

What is one to make of Meek's stories? They seem a bit far-fetched and they are impossible to verify. Should we even believe them?

First off, none of these bears appeared to be a bloodthirsty monster. Meek was charged twice, both times by bears acting in self-defense. One was a bear that he had already wounded. Another was a surprised mother bear. Even the bear that stole the bison meat seemed to be more curious and confused than predatory. Once the bear realized there were people under those greasy bedrolls, it fled. (Not far enough, as it turned out.)

In the 1800s, tall tales were considered good entertainment and the lines between fiction and non-fiction were not as distinct as we draw them today. Today, certain elements of Meek's stories seem implausible, even inconsistent. Take for example, the case of the mother bear that Meek killed in hand-to-paw combat. Why did Meek at first attempt to stab the attacking bear with a knife, when he had a far more formidable tomahawk equally at hand? Why didn't he just use the tomahawk first?

Alas, Joe is not around to ask. His times are long gone. The mountain man era may be over, but as long as the grizzly roams free, the adventure of wilderness remains.

Steel-jaw Provocation

MOST BEAR BIOLOGISTS, OLD-TIME HUNTERS, AND WILDERNESS rangers will tell you that an unprovoked grizzly bear isn't nearly as dangerous as it is made out to be. More than anything, bears want to be left alone. A *provoked* grizzly, however, is an entirely different matter. Once a grizzly is riled up, it's a formidable animal indeed. Beware of any bear with cubs and any bear that has been wounded by bullets, hit by a car, or beaten by a rival bear.

But nothing quite infuriates a grizzly bear like having its foot smashed in the spring-loaded jaws of a steel trap. In the early twentieth century, the grim tales of Montana bear trappers Slim Lynch, John Graham, and Joseph "Frenchy" Duret punctuated the following fact: A trapper out to collect the hide of a grizzly bear may pay with his own.

Today in Montana, people still occasionally set traps for bears, either to capture animals for study or to remove bears that have become too familiar around rural homes and campgrounds. Modern trappers often use big, portable box traps, called culvert traps. Culvert traps were originally built of road culverts welded on a trailer frame and hauled behind pickup trucks. Today they're custom-welded of aluminum alloys, but the name has stuck. While individual black bears can often be lured into culvert traps time and again, grizzlies often wise up and refuse to go into a culvert trap after being captured once or twice.

Bears that are too cagey for culvert traps can often be nabbed with a well-placed foot snare. These snares are made of aircraft-grade steel cable, anchored to a tree. A bear caught in a properly constructed foot snare can be drugged and released without injury, nearly every time. This doesn't mean the bears are passive. Modern trappers know first-hand the destructive fury of a trapped grizzly. Snared grizzlies sometimes vent their rage on whatever trees are within reach, biting and clawing at the trees and ground until the trap site looks as if it were dynamited.

In the early 1900s, trappers were eager to kill bears, not study them. America was in the final campaigns in a century-long war against predators. Settlers used whatever means was practical to destroy any creature that might eat a sheep, horse, or cow. Bears were shot, poisoned, and trapped along with wolves, cougars, and coyotes for what was widely considered the common good. If altruism wasn't sufficient incentive, there was the added bonus of the bounty paid for the scalp.

In the late 1800s and early 1900s, a principal weapon against bears was the Number 5 Newhouse grizzly trap—a giant steel instrument forged in Oneida, New York. Steel-jaw traps have been around for centuries with only a few modifications to their efficient and simple design. The jaws are two semi-circles of steel powered by one or two springs. The jaws are held open by a trigger called a "dog." The dog is attached to a thin metal plate called a pan. Step on the pan and the jaws snap shut so fast you cannot see it happen.

The Number 5 Newhouse is four feet long. Its open jaws spread about twenty inches across. The manufacturer provided additional bite by welding three-inch steel spikes to each jaw, slightly offset for maximum penetration into the bear's leg. The trap also "jumps" somewhat when triggered, so it clamps as high as possible on the bear's leg.

A trap's two springs store the trap's energy. On most traps, the trapper simply steps on the springs and the jaws flop open. On the Number 5 Newhouse, a 200-pound trapper could jump up and down on the springs and accomplish nothing. Instead, the trapper must use special clamps to compress the springs. That's how strong the springs are. The trap built to grab and hold a grizzly would crush a lesser creature in half.

Bear trapping is generally a matter of bait and wait. Trappers would boil a trap in a barrel to kill the human scent and then set it, buried in the duff, beside a decaying carcass. A log chain anchored the trap to a tree or log so the bear couldn't run off. But they tried. A 1900 Libby, Montana, *News* reported that one local grizzly hauled a 45-pound trap three days through the state's most dense and rugged forests. Every time the trap became hopelessly tangled in downed trees or brush, the bear would chew the interfering logs until it was free again. That same paper in 1904 reported that another trapped grizzly bear bawled for three days, creating a ruckus that people heard ten miles away. (Which seems a bit exaggerated, but one gets the idea.)

Alberta wilderness guide Andy Russell grew up in grizzly country just north of Montana. In his youth, he helped destroy stock-killing bears that were caught in steel traps. They left an impression. "Nothing fights like a grizzly in a trap," Russell wrote in his book, *Grizzly Country*. "It is the great power and the wild, free-roaming spirit of the mountain ignominiously shackled in steel... It is a kind of desecration—an obscenity. There is a lurching and a stench that does not fit the dignity of this animal."

As effective as it was, the Number 5 Newhouse had serious disadvantages. The trap plus a length of log chain weighed roughly seventy pounds and was a terrible burden to lug into the wilderness. Creative trappers found alternatives. Early trappers in forested areas built enormous "cabin traps"—essentially stout log cabins with a trap door. The cabins had portals so a trapper could poke a rifle muzzle inside the trap and kill the bear. Montana cattlemen sometimes wrapped blasting caps in burlap and honey. These deadly packages were left near carcasses where investigating animals would bite into the explosive and decapitate themselves in the ensuing explosion. There is one record of an Ennis cattleman ordering 5000 blasting caps and 200 gallons of honey for this purpose. A more widespread practice was lacing carrion with strychnine, either tablets or powder. That killed all scavengers indiscriminately, including many prized domestic dogs.

Columbia Falls trapper Slim Lynch demonstrated that another bear-killing tool carried a peril all its own. Around 1912 Lynch ran trap lines in the North Fork of the Flathead River, a broad and timbered valley that even today hosts a dense population of grizzly bears. In 1912, as today, the North Fork was habitat for fur-bearing animals such as wolves, wolverines, martens, and lynx. That winter Lynch was trapping beavers. He worked with Chance Bebee, but on this occasion Bebee had returned to town for supplies, leaving Slim alone with his dog.

Slim maintained a tiny cabin at Kishaneena Creek, just north of the United States-Canadian border, forty miles from what passed for civilization at Columbia Falls. Over the winter Slim and Bebee had amassed a sizable stash of pelts and a stack of discarded beaver carcasses. As the weather warmed into spring, the carcasses began to stink. The odor attracted a bear, hungry and lean after hibernation. Slim feared the bear would finish the beaver carcasses and then devour every edible morsel inside the cabin, wreaking havoc in the meantime.

Hauling away and burying the beaver carcasses didn't appeal to Slim. He wanted to get rid of the bear, but a steel-jaw bear trap was heavy and expensive. Slim settled on a substitute called a "set gun."

Bebee had warned Slim against the plan, but Slim was young and stubborn. To build a set-gun trap, a trapper needed only a gun, a string, and bait. First the trapper would take a spare firearm (usually an old rifle or a sawed-off shotgun) and lash it to a tree. He pointed the muzzle of the gun at a pile of bait. Then he tied a string to the trigger and stretched the string in front of the bait to work as a trip line. Finally the trapper loaded and cocked the gun, leaving the gun "set." The bear would investigate the bait, trip the line, and shoot itself at point-blank range.

Lacking a cast-off rifle or shotgun, Slim used his pistol. (Some versions of the story say it was a nine-millimeter semiautomatic Luger, while another claims it was a forty-one caliber, double-action Colt revolver.) Slim rigged the bait, set the trip line, and cocked the pistol. He returned to his cabin to await the results of his cunning.

Sometime later, Slim heard the report of the handgun, just as he hoped. He dashed outside expecting to find a dead bear. Instead, he found only the smoking pistol. Slim had positioned the gun too high so the bullet failed to hit the bear. Perhaps Slim panicked, figuring the bear would return. In a horrible fraction of a second, Slim inadvertently pulled the string still tied to the gun's trigger. The pistol fired again. The bullet ripped a dime-sized hole through Slim's groin. The bullet entered three inches below his belt buckle, glanced off the pelvis bone, and tore a ragged exit hole two inches higher in his back.

Slim staggered to the cabin. He was young and strong but badly wounded and miles from help. He tore scraps from his shirt, using the rags to plug his bullet wounds. Perhaps he believed he might survive. No one knows how long it took Slim to bleed to death on his bunk. Some time later, the bear returned to clean up the rest of the beaver carcasses. Later still, the bear investigated the scent of decay wafting from the cabin and tore down the door.

When Slim was late returning from his trapping, his friends began to worry. Then Slim's hungry dog wandered into a homestead several miles away. His friends went looking for him and found the telltale clues: The gun lashed to the tree, a pair of bloody pants on the cabin floor, human bones scattered around the cabin, along with the spoor of a bear.

Slim's friends collected what was left of the trapper in a flour sack and buried him under a stout old larch tree nearby. One might imagine Slim would have approved of such an arrangement, but not everyone thought the burial site was adequate. Slim's remains were later re-interred at a proper cemetery in Columbia Falls.

*　*　*

The same year Slim met his demise in the mossy shadows of Kishaneena Creek, a miner and market hunter named John Graham was eking out a living just north of Yellowstone National Park. The bedrock schist and gneiss near Jardine are shot through with veins of gold and silver. Jardine had been a busy mining district since the 1860s and boomed between 1904 and 1910.

In 1912 Graham was 63. The latest boom at the Crevice Mountain Mining District had petered out, but Graham was sticking to his claim. His neighbors were few and far between and Graham didn't get along with most of them anyway. In particular, Graham conducted a running feud with another woodsman named Joseph "Frenchy" Duret. Frenchy stood accused of stealing elk meat from Graham; Frenchy later fingered Graham for allegedly selling elk meat illegally. Despite their feuds in life, the two would be oddly joined by their bizarre deaths.

In a word, Graham was a sadist. A sympathetic observer might argue that life was dull in his backwoods shack, but it's difficult to justify his peculiar form of entertainment. Not content with merely trapping bears, Graham enjoyed torturing them. Specifically, when he had a bear hopelessly secured in a steel trap, he would blast it with light loads from a shotgun until the animal slowly bled to death. Evidently he enjoyed hearing their roars of outrage and pain.

In the spring of 1912, grizzlies were emerging from their winter dens. One large male grizzly found a horse carcass near Graham's claim on Crevice Mountain and fed on it. Graham replied by using the carcass as bait, setting a trap in the dirt beside it.

On May 4, Graham captured the bear. He approached the tethered animal, took aim and fired. Perhaps as Graham had planned, his first shot only enraged the bear. He shouldered his weapon and fired again. This time, Graham's plan went wrong.

The bear ripped itself free. The jaws of the trap had just nabbed the bruin by the toes of one forepaw. With a mighty yank, the bear left three bloody toes in the teeth of the trap. The enraged bear flew into Graham, swatting aside the man's rifle. The bear's claws swiped the man's throat, exposing his windpipe. A sidelong swat to Graham's head loosened his teeth, shattered his jaw, and nearly tore off his face.

Another miner named Adolph Hageman was working nearby. Hageman heard the shots and came to see what Graham had caught. Instead, he found Graham, bleeding and staggering toward Hageman's cabin. Hageman ran for the doctor in Gardiner, but the trapper was dead by the time a doctor arrived. Graham had tortured his last grizzly.

A band of local hunters and hounds trailed the wounded animal but lost it. Oddly enough, that was not the last history tells of the bear. The male's forepaw healed from its ragged amputation. The bruin became known as "Old Two Toes" and was a feature at the garbage dumps in Yellowstone National Park, where tourists by the hundreds gathered to watch bears.

As is sometimes the case with garbage-eating bears, Old Two Toes became increasingly bold and aggressive. It's also possible that the nagging pain of his wounded forepaw made the bruin cranky or made it difficult for the animal to forage on natural foods. In Yellowstone, Old Two Toes hurt two park visitors at Fishing Bridge in the heart of the park. The details of those incidents are poorly documented, but park rangers considered Old Two Toes a menace.

In the fall of 1916, four years after Graham's death, Old Two Toes must have been desperate to put on weight before winter's hibernation. On September 8, a government teamster named Frank Welch and two companions were hauling wagonloads of supplies to a road camp within Yellowstone, near Cooke City. The road was long so they camped out at Soda Butte. The freighters slept under their wagons. That night, Old Two Toes came looking for food. Oats suited the bear's fancy, so Old Two Toes climbed into Welch's wagon, ripping the canvas tarp. Welch tried to drive off the bear with pots and pans and even swung an axe at it, but the bear instead turned on him. In the confusion of darkness, Welch's companions repelled the bear with Roman candles they had packed for that purpose. As Welch tried to scramble to safety, the bear raked its two remaining claws across Welch's shoulder, breaking ribs and puncturing a lung. The man's left arm was mangled and torn and he suffered two deep lacerations across the thigh. The teamsters fought off the bear and were able to get their injured friend to assistance at Mammoth Hot Springs, but Welch died three days later.

In the meantime, roadworkers set another sort of trap for

Old Two Toes. They placed garbage over a charge of dynamite. When Old Two Toes came to dine, they blew the animal into a furry sack of broken bones.

●　　●　　●

NOW LET US REVISIT JOSEPH "FRENCHY" DURET, John Graham's neighbor and sometime rival. Frenchy was reputedly a deserter from the French military who had hewn a meadow of stumps in a lodgepole pine forest near the headwaters of Slough Creek. The skull of a bull elk stared out over the porch of the cabin Frenchy shared with his mail-order bride, Jennie McWilliams.

Slough Creek flows through the northwestern corner of Yellowstone, off the main tourist routes. It is a favorite place for visitors seeking cutthroat trout, elk herds, or the grand sweep of the park's northern mountains. Frenchy's cabin was at the very headwaters of Slough Creek, north of the national park boundary and within the state of Montana. Frenchy got by running strings of packhorses and killing whatever creatures he could sell for meat, fur, or bounty. He was not always on the same side as the law.

In June 1922, ten years after Graham's death, Frenchy tightened the clamps on yet another grizzly trap. He must have compared his plan to that of his old nemesis, John Graham. Frenchy knew the stakes of this dangerous game. Given human nature, Frenchy must have reasoned why he would not share Graham's fate. Frenchy probably assured himself that he was a more careful trapper, a better shot, and a wiser woodsman. After all, he wasn't out to torment bears but simply kill them.

When Frenchy checked his trapline, he found a bear anchored in one of the traps. He returned to his cabin for his rifle and to tell Jennie. Frenchy loaded his rifle, called up his dog, and returned to the trapped bear. The bear was another large specimen, probably a male. Frenchy's task was to approach near enough for a sure, killing shot, but not so close as to be within reach of the bear.

The bear saw Frenchy coming. More likely, it heard or smelled Frenchy long before the trapper came into view. When Frenchy closed in, the animal lunged. The chain broke.

The bear came on fast, barely slowed by the 50-pounds of steel clamped firmly to one paw. Frenchy had time to fire one frantic, useless shot. The bear slapped Frenchy down, lashing him with its claws and digging his teeth deep into the man's body. The bear turned its fury on Frenchy's rifle, biting great chunks from the stock and scarring the steel barrel. Frenchy's dog lit into the bear in retaliation, tearing out clumps of fur. Finally the bear left, dragging the great black trap into the forest.

Frenchy emerged from the attack covered in dirt, blood, and pine needles. He was hurt badly and knew he needed help if he were to survive. In shock and pain and weakened by blood loss, Frenchy dragged himself toward his cabin. Jennie was his only hope.

Meanwhile, Jennie grew worried and went for help. The next day Yellowstone National Park buffalo keeper Peck Hutchins and ranger William Denhoff went looking for Frenchy. They found him, dead, about a mile and a half from the trap site. He had crawled all the distance, leaving most of his blood on the trail behind him.

The men explored the trap site, compiling enough evidence to re-create the scene. The ranger and buffalo keeper buried Frenchy a half-mile from where they found him. The only other attendant at the wilderness funeral was his widow, Jennie.

The bear was never heard from again. Years later, though, a wanderer along the banks of Slough Creek stumbled across a rusty and gnarled piece of steel. It was Frenchy's bear trap. It was a relic of the Old West—an artifact the kinds of which are now found in museums and on barroom walls.

* * *

OVER THE YEARS, most western states destroyed their grizzly bears. The last grizzly in Texas was killed in 1890, North Dakota in 1897, Nevada in 1907, California in 1922, Oregon in 1931 and Arizona in 1935. Frank Clark, a clever trapper who placed his trap in a bear wallow, killed the last grizzly in Utah in 1923. That same year the Montana Legislature classified the grizzly bear as a game animal to be managed more like deer and elk than predator pests like coyotes. This was one of the first steps to conserve grizzly bears in North America. One of the side effects of the new law was that trappers could no longer lay steel for the great bear.

The Night of Terror That Changed Everything

THAT EVENING ON THE CONTINENTAL DIVIDE THE MOUNTAIN LIGHT was tinted copper with the airborne smoke of distant forest fires. It had been an usually dry summer. When thunderstorms ripped through the high country, they delivered lightning but no rain. The trail dust was dry as talcum. The leaves on huckleberry bushes were brittle and brown. Everything in the forest seemed primed to burn. In Glacier National Park, the potential for forest fires was on everyone's mind, but by the morning of August 13, 1967, a tragic shock would distract everyone from the blazes.

Roy Ducat and Julie Hegelson were on a break from their summer jobs at East Glacier Lodge, a historic railroad hotel in the southeast corner of the park. Roy was 18 years old but already a sophomore studying biology at Bowling Green University in his native Ohio. This summer, he worked bussing dirty dishes at the lodge. Julie was 19, from Eden Prairie, Minnesota. She ran mountains of sheets, towels, and tablecloths through the hotel laundry. The work was demanding and the days long. Now, toward the end of the summer, they were enjoying a couple of days off.

The couple hitchhiked to Logan Pass, the highest point in the park accessible by car. The sweeping landscape of glacially carved limestone was a breathtaking change from their homes in the American Midwest. Logan Pass is six thousand feet above sea level, where the forest of steeple-shaped subalpine fir gives way to lush alpine meadows. Above the meadows, the mountains emerge as bare rock, sharp and jagged as broken bone. Even at this normally cool elevation, that scorching August brought a string of afternoons near 90 degrees.

Roy and Julie walked seven-and-a-half miles along the Highline Trail to a small plateau called Granite Park. The hike rambled with stunning views every step. Nearly the entire trail is above timberline, but the hike lacks the lung-busting climbs that can make mountain travel an unpleasant chore. Still, it was a demanding trek, particularly for the young campers hauling packs of overnight gear in the afternoon heat.

One reward at the end of the hike is the Granite Park Chalet, a Swiss-style backcountry inn built of local stone. In 1967 people with enough money could spend the night between clean sheets and be served fine meals. Folks on a lower budget, like Roy and Julie, could treat themselves to the chalet's pie and coffee before moving on to the campground a quarter-mile away. The chalet offered comfort in the wilderness, but there was another attraction here: Granite Park was known as one of the best places in Glacier to see grizzly bears.

Roy and Julie arrived at the chalet about seven o'clock in the evening, late in the day but still a couple of hours before the sun set behind the smoky western haze. After a short rest to marvel at Heaven's Peak, the couple continued downhill to the Granite Park Campground. Given the hot and unbroken weather, Roy and Julie did not even bother with a tent. Besides, the stars glimmered overhead. They just rolled their sleeping bags over the ground and stared into the vast and marvelous void.

Shortly after falling asleep, Roy jolted awake. He heard an animal in the forest. He laughed when he finally saw it: It was a squirrel. He got up, walked to the creek for a sip of water, then returned to his sleeping bag and dropped back into unconsciousness. No one had ever been killed by a bear in Glacier National Park—why should he worry?

· · ·

THE STORY, sometimes called The Night of the Grizzlies, often begins at this point—the night of August 13, 1967. But in fact, the story begins decades before Roy and Julie were even born. The story stretches back to 1910, when railroad tycoon James J. Hill and New York magazine editor George B. Grinnell convinced Congress to set aside a million mountainous acres as Glacier National Park. Hill had amassed a fortune hauling goods across the Rocky Mountains. Now he stood to profit by hauling sightseers into them.

Those sightseers needed shelter. In the decade before World War I, Hill (and later his son, Louis) financed the construction of a string of ritzy hotels along his Great Northern Railroad. The East Glacier Lodge, with its massive columns of coastal Douglas fir, was one of them. In those days, Glacier had few roads and hiking wasn't fashionable, so Louis Hill built a string of backcountry chalets accessible by horses.

Each summer, well-to-do tourists arrived by passenger trains and took horseback trips through the mountains. Those who went to Granite Park Chalet found food fit for mountain appetites. After meals, the leftover fruit rinds, stale bread, fish bones, meat gristle, grease from the range, and other scraps were piled into a heap 200 feet from the chalet. At sundown, bears would troop out of the forest and clean up the garbage, thrilling visitors from Seattle, Chicago, and Minneapolis. Bears served both as wilderness theater and as quadruped garbage disposals. At the end of the season, just before snow closed the mountain passes, crews opened up the chalet sewage tanks and drained the contents across the ground. Although there were no tourists around to watch, the bears ate up that mess as well.

Over the decades, park visitors changed habits. After World War II, the popularity of cars and trailers made motor campgrounds more popular and more affordable than horseback treks. In the 1960s, lightweight camping gear made backpacking attractive. One by one, Hill's chalets were closed, razed, and burned. Eventually only two chalets remained, the two which happened to be built of stone. One was near Sperry Glacier, the other at Granite Park.

At Granite Park, the evening bear show remained largely unchanged. By the 1960s there was a trash burner at the chalet, but it couldn't handle all the waste. Sometimes visitors would drop morsels to the bears from the chalet balcony. Feeding bears was against the rules, but the rules were often overlooked. Besides, the tourists so enjoyed the bears.

*   *   *

IF YOU OR I HAD ARRIVED at Granite Park Campground that evening in 1967, we would have smelled the balsam scent of subalpine fir, the odor of pies and coffee at the chalet, and the smoke of distant forest fires. A grizzly bear would have smelled all those aromas and a thousand more. A bear depends on scent the way humans depend on light. Wave after wave of invisible molecules streams information into its brain. A bear's nose tells it what is in order in its world and what is amiss.

Some things were in order that day: The human beings, so seasonal in their mountain habits, would remain in the high country for another two weeks or so. Until then, they still left fresh garbage mounded behind the chalet. Bears would loaf away these hot summer afternoons in some shadowy tangle of brush and visit the dump as the evening grew cool. That day, perhaps six grizzlies lingered near the chalet.

As the bears lumbered out of the forest, the humans lined up on the balcony of the chalet. Others perched on the roof, holding their cameras at ready. Their flash bulbs popped in bursts.

A female bear knew her place in the social order of the bears and joined the feed when it was her turn, not wanting to risk her two cubs to the wrath of an angry male. The bear sniffed for her dinner as her mother had taught her and her grandmother had taught her mother.

Perhaps something was out of order that August night. Earlier in the summer chalet visitors reported seeing violent clashes between grizzly bears vying for territory in the pile of garbage. Perhaps the female bear was not receiving as much food as usual. Perhaps the unnatural diet of cooked and discarded food had left her underweight for the approaching winter. Maybe the unnatural concentrations of refined sugar had damaged her teeth, or the injury on her rear paw nagged her with pain.

Or perhaps it was just a night of extraordinarily bad luck.

Camped out under the stars, Julie heard the bear first. Probably the bear approached with a typical, huffing shuffle, following her nose and not worrying about making too much noise. The bear was not stalking Julie in the literal sense. The bear was curious, foraging, and came across Julie in her sleeping bag. Above all, the bear was hungry. Two cubs drained her energy. Winter was coming.

Julie could smell the bear's musk and the odor of burnt garbage as the animal approached. No doubt, the bear smelled her. The bear sniffed the edges of her sleeping bag. The bear may have smelled traces of sandwiches Roy had stashed under a nearby log or the leftover food he had buried. Perhaps the bear smelled the candy bar in Roy's pack, or the lipstick, bug spray, and chewing gum in Julie's bag. Perhaps, as the bear's heavy breath hit her, Julie uttered a silent prayer. Or a curse of fear. Julie woke Roy with a hissing whisper, *"Don't move."*

Roy shook off his sleep and awoke to a real nightmare. He found himself in the presence of something he could only identify as large and dark. A bear was a few feet away. In 1967 the official advice about what to do in the case of a bear attack was simple: Play dead. The advice worked, at least some of the time. But the effectiveness of this strategy depends entirely on the circumstances of a given attack. These were not the circumstances.

The bear's initial blow knocked the two campers five feet out of their unzipped sleeping bags. The bear was not particularly large—about 265 pounds—but displayed the amazing strength of her species. The bear first tore into Roy, biting and chewing his shoulder. While listening to the bear's teeth grate against his bones, Roy clenched his own teeth, trying with all his might to play dead and praying the bear would drop him and go away.

The bear did drop Roy but turned to Julie, biting her horribly in the throat and chest. She willed herself to remain still and silent. She fought all her instincts of panic. Finally, Roy heard her pleading. *"It hurts,"* she whispered. *"It hurts."*

Realizing the futility of lying still for this punishment, Julie gave up the passive strategy. She shrieked: "Someone help us!" Her screams were so loud they woke up people staying in the chalet, hundreds of yards away behind stone walls. One visitor snapped awake thinking a woman outside was being raped.

When Julie began to scream, the bear clamped its jaws upon the woman and ran, dragging her over rocks and through brush. Stunned and agonized, Roy listened as her screams grew faint. Finally, Julie went silent. Roy remained, bleeding, terrified, and alone. It was about one o'clock in the morning. The sun would not rise for six hours.

•   •   •

TO UNDERSTAND WHY BEARS OCCASIONALLY ATTACK and kill people, one must understand something about bears. Basically, specialists put bear aggression in two categories: Genetic predisposition and learned behavior.

Genetic predisposition refers to inherited behavioral traits. Every animal has an internal switch that flicks to "fight" or "flight" during a stressful situation. A mother grizzly bear is notorious for her willingness to defend her cubs, a trait that well served her ancestors over millions of years in an Ice Age tundra loaded with dangerous predators. But aggression as a learned behavior is quite different.

For any animal, survival in the wild is largely a problem of obtaining and conserving precious energy. Conflict is an inherently stressful process that drains energy. This is one reason most grizzly bears give humans a wide berth. We simply aren't worth the energy of being around. As grizzly expert Dr. Charles Jonkel says, most bears are "polite." They avoid conflict 99.99 percent of the time.

But bears can learn to overrule their natural caution and their tendency to avoid conflict, particularly if they are rewarded with food. Since a bear sleeps for six months, it must eat an entire year's worth of food in half-a-year's time. If food and people are in the same place, most bears avoid the food, at least for a time. Gradually a particularly bold bear may creep in, perhaps at night, to sample the food. If the food is good, the bear will return.

Once rewarded, the bear will likely become bolder and bolder. Perhaps it will visit the food source during the day, instead of at night. After a time, the bear may encounter people. If the bear receives no negative reinforcement, the bear will think, in effect, *That wasn't so bad.* The reward of food outweighed the risk of lingering around humans. Once emboldened, the bear will return as long as the food remains available, tolerating more and more contact with people.

In extreme situations, bears connect the dots. That is, they learn that where there are people, there is bound to be food. They will begin to seek out people. At Granite Park Chalet, this progressed to the point that people would stand on the balcony and feed full-grown, wild grizzly bears by hand. This pattern continued at Granite Park over fifty years, over three or four generations of grizzly bears. Mother bears taught cubs to include Granite Park Chalet as part of their late-summer feeding circuit: Marmot burrows, here. Huckleberry patch, here. Glacier lily roots, here. Garbage heap, here. If you don't get full, sniff around until you find a second helping.

Roy and Julie had food and cosmetics near their campsite. These scents may have attracted the bear. That night, the bear was hungry or curious enough to sample a potential new food—human beings.

◦ ◦ ◦

Bleeding and terrified, Roy rose to his feet and staggered to a neighboring camp. Campers tore a cot out of a nearby patrol cabin and made a stretcher to carry him up to the chalet. Their shouts, along with Julie's original screams, woke up everyone at the chalet. That included a National Park Service seasonal naturalist named Joan Devereaux. She was trained in giving nature talks, not facing down man-eaters. She grabbed the chalet's radio and contacted a fire camp. She wanted backup. She requested someone fly in immediately with a rifle and medical supplies.

Roy was in for a badly needed piece of good luck: Three physicians were staying at the chalet, including a surgeon. After examining Roy, the doctors figured his left arm was broken and he had severe lacerations on the arm, shoulder, and lower back. They tried to staunch the bleeding until the helicopter arrived. Other guests built bonfires, lit lanterns, and waved flashlights to direct the pilot into a landing zone behind the chalet.

At one-forty-five in the morning, helicopter pilot John Westover touched down behind the chalet. The Bell 3GB-1 helicopter dropped off Ranger Gary Bunney, who carried plasma, extra bandages, and a .300 Winchester magnum rifle. The helicopter was not outfitted with a stretcher, so the doctors belted Roy into the passenger seat. A half-hour after setting down, Westover took off again, whisking Roy to the hospital in Kalispell where the he would undergo three hours of surgery. He would spend nine days in the hospital, but he would survive.

In spite of shock and blood loss, Roy remained conscious during the entire ordeal at the chalet. He was nearly frantic for Julie. The others promised they would go look for her.

Ranger Bunney rallied a posse of ten nervous volunteers and threw together a plan. Someone built a bonfire in a tin washtub that could be carried. By that crude light, a few flashlights, lanterns, and a dim moon, they plunged into the night. The searchers found the campsite a wreck of debris. Shoes, sleeping bags, and gear were strewn about. What's more, an obvious trail of blood reflected the lantern light. They followed the blood 225 feet downslope and the sign disappeared. They continued in the general direction another sixty-five feet. From there, they heard a faint cry. Fifty feet further downslope, the searchers found Julie, face down and covered with blood. They rolled her over. She was breathing, but barely.

The posse hauled Julie back to the chalet on the cot spring and radioed the helicopter to return. Julie was laid on a table inside the chalet's dining hall. The three doctors did what they could to keep Julie alive as she labored to breathe with a badly torn throat and ribcage. Although barely conscious, Julie moved several times and muttered, *It hurts.* As it turned out, the only guest who could do anything for Julie was a Catholic priest named Father Connolly, who tried to give comfort as Julie slipped into death. By the time the helicopter landed at Granite Park Chalet for a second time that night, there was nothing left to be done for Julie.

Warren L. Hanna, author of *The Grizzlies of Glacier,* figures the odds of Julie being killed by a grizzly bear were at least a million to one. Such figures are difficult to calculate. Up until that time, Glacier had hosted 15 million visitors and none had been killed by a bear.

It's also difficult to calculate the attack's impact on the collective psyche of everyone associated with Glacier. The horror was immeasurable. Now multiply that terror by two. As Julie's body was flown out of the wilderness, another band of backpackers was suffering through a nightmare of its own.

●　●　●

Trout Lake fills a glacial trough in the Camas Creek Drainage. It's about eight air miles from Granite Park Chalet but several thousand feet lower in elevation. Dense Douglas fir surrounds the lake, and the steep slopes are scarred with avalanche chutes. To reach Trout Lake, one must hike three and a half miles over Howe Ridge. As one might guess by its name, Trout Lake is a popular place to catch fish, take a quick swim, and enjoy the sunshine sparkling on the water.

That was the goal of five young hikers who walked from Lake McDonald to Trout Lake on August 12. Like Roy and Julie, these five were seasonal workers for the park's chief concessionaire, Glacier Park Inc. Arizona native Ron Noseck, 21, worked as a waiter at the same East Glacier Lodge as Roy and Julie. His 23-year-old brother, Ray, worked at Lake McDonald Lodge on the park's west side. They were joined by two California women, Denise Huckle, 20, who worked at East Glacier Lodge, and Michele Koons, 19, who sold trinkets at the gift shop at Lake McDonald Lodge. The youngest member of the hike was a Minnesota boy, Paul Dunn, 16, who bussed tables at East Glacier Lodge. They also picked up a stray puppy along the trail.

The group planned to continue several miles upstream from Trout Lake to Arrow Lake. But on their way they met a pair of fishermen—a father and a son—who had been to Arrow Lake earlier that day. While at Arrow Lake, the two had been approached by an aggressive grizzly bear. The bear seemed stunted, rangy, and unusually bold. The animal chased the father and son up separate trees, keeping them there for hours as it rummaged through their packsacks and ate their stringer of trout. Eventually, the bear shuffled away into the forest and the pair dropped from the trees and headed home.

The young band of five hikers scrapped their plans to camp at Arrow Lake. Instead, they would proceed no farther than Trout Lake. Unfortunately, the choice would not make a bit of difference.

The five found a flat spot near the shore of Trout Lake, unrolled their sleeping bags, and went fishing. Michele stayed at camp, playing with the puppy while the others fished. At eight in the evening, everyone returned to camp, built a fire, and roasted hotdogs. As they ate, Michele saw the grizzly. "Here comes a bear," she said. Everyone looked up.

The bear came utterly without fear. At Michele's warning, the campers dropped everything and backed away from camp.

The bear continued into camp as if it were invited. The hikers retreated fifty yards and watched as the bear casually walked from plate to plate, licking each clean and sniffing for more. The campers drove off the bear with rocks before it totally cleaned out their food.

The group considered abandoning camp altogether, but their

options were limited. They had only one weak flashlight, so going anywhere in the dark would be difficult, if not dangerous. There was a campers shelter at Arrow Lake, but they knew it was full. They considered making a break for Lake McDonald, but that would mean repeating the day's long hike in the dark.

Instead, they retreated to the lakeshore near a large logjam. They built a fire—large as they could make it—and were determined to keep it blazing all nightlong. They arranged their sleeping bags in a half-circle around it, flanked on one side by the fire and on the other by darkness. They managed a bit of sleep. They heard the bear splashing in the shallows of the lake and built up the fire. One by one, they drifted into exhausted sleep. At four-thirty in the morning, the fire died down. The bear returned.

The campers tried to play dead in hopes the animal would leave them alone. The bear approached young Paul Dunn, sniffing at his still body. The bear took Paul's sleeping bag in its mouth and ripped it open. The bear's next swipe tore the sweatshirt off Paul's back.

Paul had enough of playing dead. He stood and fled for the trees, shouting for the others to do the same. In the dark and confusion, four campers scrambled high enough into trees to escape the bear's reach. All climbed for their lives, except Michelle. Her friends strained to see her by the glow of the campfire's coals: She remained in her sleeping bag. Perhaps Michelle was petrified with fear. Perhaps she was still trying to play dead. Perhaps the zipper on her sleeping bag was jammed.

As Michele's friends screamed for her to join them in the trees, she screamed back that she could not. The bear took the sleeping bag in its jaws and began to drag Michele away in a bundle. Goose down billowed from the torn bag. Her friends pleaded with her to unzip the bag and escape. She screamed that she could not—the zipper was in the bear's mouth. The bear dragged Michele into the forest and turned its attention from the bag to the woman. Helpless in their trees, her friends heard every detail of Michele's hopeless struggle.

"It's got my arm off," she moaned. "Oh my God. I'm dead."

• • •

AT DAWN, the four remaining hikers dropped to the ground. They were cold and cramped from an hour and a half in the trees and returned as fast as they could to the trailhead. They did not know what had become of Michele, but they were too terrified to look for her without help. They hiked back over Howe Ridge to Lake McDonald where they found rangers. Still dumbfounded over the Granite Park attacks, park officials realized they had an entirely new disaster to attend to.

Two of the young backpackers, Ron Noseck and Paul Dunn, hiked back to the attack scene with seasonal ranger Leonard Landa. Seasonal ranger Bert Gildart hustled after them, catching up at Trout Lake. The four spread out in the woods and began searching. They followed a short trail of goose down, blood, and bits of cloth. Landa found Michele's body about a hundred feet from where she had camped. Unlike Julie at Granite Park, Michele Koons had been partially consumed.

Just as the four found Michele's body, they heard a helicopter landing nearby. It was pilot Westover, landing for another terrible mauling.

Rangers Gildart and Landa had an immediate suspect. One skinny bear had earned a reputation that summer at Kelly Camp, a cluster of private inholdings on Lake McDonald. The bear had been eating garbage, breaking into cabins, tearing apart backpacks, and bullying food from hikers and campers. Several park visitors reported being frightened when the bear followed them on trails.

Landa and Gildart took up rifles and cleared campers out

of Trout and Arrow lakes. They found the Arrow Lake hikers' shelter full of six campers, some of whom had experienced trouble with the same bear. Landa and Gildart escorted the group out the woods, then turned around and returned to the backcountry.

Two days after the attack, Gildart and Landa were at the Arrow Lake shelter. The rangy, unusually bold bear approached within twenty yards. They shot it dead. Immediately examining the carcass, they noted blood in the claws and fur. Later, park biologist Cliff Martinka flew to the scene. He cut open the bear's stomach and found some of Michele's hair inside. A Federal Bureau of Investigation laboratory confirmed that initial evidence.

The bear was a 17-year-old female. She was not particularly old, but she was emaciated. Furthermore, she had shards of glass imbedded in her teeth. Over the years she had learned to live off campground trash, but the unnatural diet had left her in a pathetic condition. Like the bear at Granite Park, the Trout Lake bear had blurred the line between food and humans until the two became indistinguishable.

◦   ◦   ◦

At Granite Park, the hunt for the killer bear proved more problematic.

From his hospital room in Kalispell, Roy couldn't tell rangers if a black or a grizzly bear had attacked him; he didn't really know the difference even under the best circumstances. Rangers had little clue which bear killed Julie and attacked Roy.

Park rangers, by training, legal mandate, and personal disposition, are not eager to kill animals. But rangers began killing bears that frequented the chalet dump. Over several days they shot five bears, eventually determining the most likely suspect was an old sow with two cubs. The bear was of normal weight but had badly-worn teeth and a lacerated paw. Unlike the bear at Trout Lake, however, hard proof of the bear's guilt was never found.

*   *   *

IN A 2001 INTERVIEW, Glacier Chief Ranger Steve Frye said the night in 1967 had ripple effects, not just in Glacier but in all national parks. Between 1910 and 1966, only ten people had been seriously injured by grizzly bears in Glacier and none of them had been killed. In the 94 years before 1967, only three people had been killed by grizzly bears in any American national park, and no fatal attack was particularly recent.

In 1967 feeding bears was technically against park rules, but those rules were not aggressively enforced. In many national parks black bears begged along the highways and feeding them was widely considered harmless fun. Or nearly harmless, anyway. Every summer scores of visitors were scratched and bitten by spoiled bears.

"People thought it was just great that they could feed a cookie to a bear, or take a picture of their son on the back of a bear," Frye said. "In 1967 the agency came to the big realization that bears can and will kill people."

Glacier officials had received at least fifteen complaints about the Trout Lake before the fatal attack. Just two days before Michele was killed, the bear had run a troop of local Girl Scouts out of the Trout Lake Campground, eating the potatoes the girls left behind as they ran.

Another big change in the 1960s and '70s was the growing interest in wilderness hiking. When it was established in 1910, Glacier received just a few thousand visitors, and few of those penetrated the backcountry. By 1967, roughly one million people visited Glacier annually and backpacking was a new fad.

Immediately after the attack, some observers speculated the

two attacks were triggered by some environmental factor: The drought, forest fires, lightning, and a poor crop of huckleberries. After thirty years of research, these factors seem insignificant, Frye said. Droughts, forest fires, lightning, and periodic huckleberry crop failures are common in the northern Rockies and don't turn bears homicidal. Today Frye and most experts believe the twin attacks were simply a dumbfounding example of coincidence.

However, Frye and other experts say it was no coincidence that the bears were rummaging through the campgrounds in the first place. The bears were looking for food. Stephen Herrero, North America's foremost expert on bear attacks, says both maulings were as avoidable as they were tragic. Human actions over the decades—the intentional and unintentional feeding of bears—made the bears unnaturally dangerous.

Ranger Gildart says today it's hard to imagine how filthy Glacier's backcountry campgrounds were in the late 1960s. It was common for campers to leave leftover dinner or food they didn't want to carry. A week after the attack at Trout Lake, Gildart returned with another ranger. They filled *seventeen* burlap sacks full of garbage that had accumulated over the years.

In the weeks after the attacks, rangers began cleaning up backcountry campgrounds throughout Glacier. They began aggressively enforcing the rules against backcountry litter. Over the years, backpackers have learned to keep a clean camp. "Leave no trace" camping is now a point of pride.

"Given today's exemplary backcountry conditions, I don't think anyone can really appreciate what a God-awful situation existed prior to 1967," Gildart said thirty-four years after the attacks. "I remember seeing an extraordinary amount of garbage at Lincoln Lake, Old Man Lake, Elizabeth Lake, Trout Lake, and many others. As a result, bears had become habituated to the presence of people by virtue of their association with garbage."

The problem of grizzly bears eating garbage was by no means new in national parks. Naturalists had complained about garbage-bum bears in Yellowstone since the turn of the twentieth century. Warnings in Glacier came as early as 1919 when naturalist Enos Mills warned that bears in Glacier risked becoming "demoralized" garbage bears, like those in Yellowstone. "The grizzly bear situation in the Yellowstone is a serious and even alarming one," he wrote in 1919, "and what exists there is certain to develop in other Parks." It would take nearly fifty years and the deaths of two young women before the nation shared Mills' sense of alarm.

Today, visitors to Glacier and other national parks are warned over and over against leaving food unattended. Rangers write tickets and impose fines. All garbage at Granite Park and Sperry chalets must promptly be hauled out. After a lawsuit in 1992 filed by the Sierra Club, Glacier stopped the annual release of chalet sewage onto the nearby alpine slopes. All backcountry campsites in Glacier are equipped with bear-resistant metal boxes or suspension systems where food, toiletries, and cosmetics must be kept out of the reach of bears. Garbage bins in park communities have self-closing lids that deter bears. Picnickers and campers are warned that leaving so much as a water bottle or cookstove unattended on an outdoor table will land them a fine. Today, begging bears are rarely seen, and, overall, the number of visitors injured by bears in Glacier has decreased markedly.

Since 1967 park rangers have also refined their recommendations for what to do if a bear attacks. What works in a surprise encounter on a trail does not work with a camp-raiding bear. The advice for surviving a bear's charge during a surprise encounter is to stand your ground. Use pepper spray if you have time. If the bear continues its charge, drop to a protective, face-down position. Stay still and quiet and the bear will probably determine you're not a threat and leave.

On the other hand, if the bear—any bear, black or grizzly— comes into your camp and tries to drag you away, do not play dead. Resist. Shout. Punch. Empty your can of pepper spray down the bear's nose. It's time to fight for your life.

Still, The Night of the Grizzlies was not the last fatal bear attack in Glacier. From 1967 to 2001, bears killed ten park visitors. Of those, six people died in similar circumstances as Julie and Michele—killed at night, dragged from their sleeping bags by bears with a habit of eating human food. Frye says these statistics largely reflect the trend that more and more people are venturing into grizzly country.

Nonetheless, the odds of being killed by a Glacier bear remain infinitesimally small (roughly one death per five million visitors, given recent park visitation rates). In Glacier, cars have killed far more visitors than bears. Every death is a tragedy, but those that involve food-conditioned bears are doubly tragic, because such deaths are avoidable.

The ultimate irony of August 13, 1967, is that neither Michele nor Julie intentionally fed the bears that killed them. They paid the price for the sloppy, thoughtless, and ignorant habits of those who came before them. It is a lesson still valid in bear country today.

Public Enemy No. 1

GEORGE OSTROM IS A CLASSIC MONTANA JOURNALIST, EQUALLY comfortable in the wilderness as he is behind his typewriter or microphone. In 1975, he ran the *Kalispell Weekly News,* a colorful community newspaper that he sprinkled with wildlife photographs and biting commentary. The obituaries were called "On to the Great Reward," while marriage announcements were under the headline "The Hitching Post." A former smokejumper, Ostrom launched into stories with a similar, all-or-nothing gusto.

Ostrom's family owned a backwoods cabin between the Bob Marshall Wilderness and Glacier National Park, near where U.S. Highway 2 slices over the Continental Divide. It's in the Middle Fork of the Flathead River drainage, which includes tributaries such as Giefer Creek, Silvertip Creek, and Bear Creek. These last two streams are particularly well named, as they drain some excellent grizzly bear habitat.

It's tough country. Between Glacier National Park and Flathead National Forest, these mountains make up a couple of million acres of public wilderness, divided by a string of private cabins along the highway. The cabins are generally used on weekends during the summer and fall, remaining locked up during the week and through the winter.

In June 1975, the Middle Fork of the Flathead River flooded

in a great flush of slushy water. High water blasted out the bridge at Giefer Creek, where the Ostrom family had their cabin. When Ostrom and his son, Shannon, wanted to see how the structure had fared, they borrowed horses to ford the frigid stream. When they arrived at the cabin, they found all the windows shattered and the windowsills splintered. Shards of broken dishes were on the floor. The wood stove was tipped on its side, spilling ashes. A cot was collapsed. The cause wasn't snow or flood.

Cat burglars prowl by stealth. Bear burglars operate by brute strength. They seem equal parts thieves and vandals. Heaping a big, brown insult on top of injury, the burglar of Ostrom's cabin left a heap of dung on the floor. It was the bear's message that the animal considered this cabin his territory.

The break-in was not entirely a surprise. A bear had already raided several other cabins in the Middle Fork and had invaded a nearby Forest Service ranger station. Surveying the hundreds of dollars in damage to his cabin, Ostrom knew two things for sure: This was one hell of a mess and this was one hell of a story. Back at his *Kalispell Weekly News,* Ostrom wrote of the incident with great detail and his usual ironic wit. But the raided cabin was just the beginning. Over the next two years, the Giefer Creek grizzly would surprise even a veteran storyteller like Ostrom.

◦　◦　◦

THE GIEFER CREEK BEAR was a broad-skulled male weighing just under 400 pounds. He wasn't particularly big, nor was he particularly cantankerous. He was not known to kill livestock or threaten people. Still, Giefer became perhaps the most notorious grizzly bear in modern Montana. The *Hungry Horse News* of Columbia Falls dubbed him "the Flathead's Public Enemy No. 1."

The Giefer Creek bear began making headlines in 1975, the same year grizzly bears were listed as "threatened" under the brand-new Endangered Species Act. The Giefer bear survived just as his ancestors had: He roamed the mountain wilderness, eating as much as he could find, then sleeping through the harsh mountain winters. To him, food was food. He wasn't fussy. The only problem was finding enough.

The Giefer bear probably found human food left behind in fishing camps and rural dumps in the Middle Fork country. From there, he began to sniff around backwoods cabins. He was rewarded with scraps of trash, perhaps a garbage feast or two. For the first ten years of his life, the Giefer bear survived in secret. Then he discovered that cabins hid motherlodes of calories, free for the taking.

Imagine life from the bear's eyes: A bear could pick berries or dig roots, one at a time. But the woods were full of these big, conveniently located, wooden boxes, each one chock full of tasty bear chow. Why wouldn't he invite himself to the feast? Sure, the people might object, but then, the ants didn't like it when he licked up an anthill, either. With a little caution, he could avoid the pesky two-leggeds. Once he figured that out, raiding cabins became a favorite foraging technique, and from then on, the bear was on a collision course with mankind. The only question was, how much hell would he raise in the meantime?

Middle Fork residents were fed up with this bear's destructive habits. State Fish and Game game wardens Lornie Diest, Dave Wedum and Lou Kis had a job on their hands—get the bear away from the cabins before someone got hurt or before the bear got shot. Wardens set a culvert trap between Ostrom's cabin and a neighbor's place. The bear walked around the trap and broke into Ostrom's cabin again, repeating his destruction inside.

Kis responded by setting a foot snare, which he hid on the ground near another cabin. Days later, Kis received a phone call that a bear was in his snare. He arrived at the scene to find a gawking crowd of locals. Kis's air-powered dart gun had a leaky cylinder and wasn't particularly reliable. He took one look at the trapped bear and added a new worry to his list: The snare had only caught the bear by a few toes. The crowd was growing. If the bear slipped the snare it would probably run away, but the resulting confusion would be dangerous for bear and human alike.

Kis's leaky air rifle launched the first dart weakly toward the bear. Then he fired a second. It took Kis three darts of Sernalyn to immobilize the bear. After placing tags on the bear's ears and tattooing an identification number on its lip, he loaded the drugged bear into a culvert trap. Kis hauled the bear out of the Middle Fork and up the South Fork of the Flathead River, driving the bear about as far away from Giefer Creek as he could, about one hundred miles by road but perhaps half of that as the crow flies, or as the bear walks. Ostrom went along, snapping photographs of the bear recovering from the drug. In the next edition of his newspaper, Ostrom wrote an article titled "Giefer Creek Grizzly: The Bear That Couldn't Cope." Ostrom observed, "He is a big bear and we probably haven't heard the last of him."

Oh no. Not by a long shot.

*　*　*

THE HOMING INSTINCTS of a grizzly bear are amazing. Big male bears seem to be the best at orienteering. Bears have found their ways home after being released more than a hundred air miles from their home range. The joke among game wardens is that the bear will probably be back home before the warden makes it home with his pickup. It's only a small exaggeration.

In the summer of 1976, a year after Kis had moved the Giefer bear far up the South Fork, the grizzly was back in the Middle Fork. Moreover, he was back to his old habits, busting into cabins and ransacking the interiors for edibles. He seemed particularly fond of Smucker's strawberry jam.

Cabin owners turned their cabins into fortresses. They drove spikes through planks and then fixed these bristling barricades over doors and windows. This trick will deter most bears, but the Giefer griz learned to flatten the spikes and rip his way into the cabin. Most maddeningly, the bear seemed to be needlessly destructive. He would often go in through a door or window, but once inside he would tear his way out through a wall. Imagine the power of that—standing inside a room and ripping a new exit with your bare hands.

Wardens set more snares and, once again, caught the Giefer griz. Wardens figured the bear was irredeemable. They expected to be told to destroy it.

So they were surprised when they received their orders: They were to put a radio collar on the bear, haul him up the North Fork, and release the bear at Whale Creek. They shook their heads: The decision seemed the apex of bureaucratic stupidity. On a human scale, the North Fork seemed remote enough. Indeed, it's probably one of the most remote places in the lower forty-eight states. But the North Fork is full of cabins, just like the ones up the Middle Fork. The Giefer bear would figure that out soon enough. They bounced up the Whale Creek road and let the bear go.

The wardens hatched a plan. Maybe by keeping the Giefer bear well fed, they could keep him out of trouble. They delivered grizzly groceries in the form of road-killed deer, elk, and cattle and left them in a remote heap away from North Fork cabins. The idea was to keep the bear satiated on red meat, to keep its mind off cabins and their jars of Smucker's strawberry jam. Warden Dave Wedum remembers spending much of that summer pounding his pickup truck over the dreaded washboard of the North Fork Road, delivering load after load of stinky, maggoty carcasses.

The bear, it turned out, was ungrateful for Wedum's efforts and turned up its nose at the government's offerings. Instead, Giefer went back to hitting cabins. He had amassed a sizable record of destruction up the Middle Fork but he really got rolling up the North Fork. Before long Giefer had busted up fifteen cabins. Then his tally climbed to twenty-five.

North Fork property owners were furious. Their anger doubled when they recalled that state wardens had released the offending bear. Newspapers had a field day. The wardens felt political heat like a blast furnace. It wasn't their idea to release the bear up the North Fork—that order had come from headquarters in Helena. But wardens like Wedum and Kis had to follow orders and toe the agency line.

"I remember one woman walked into Fish and Game headquarters and she just tore into whoever was standing there," said Wedum. "I'm telling you she was not using lady-like language. She only calmed down after we called the police. Then she left."

Residents complained to their Legislators. The Legislators controlled the purse strings of the Fish and Game Department. Now the agency pulled out all the stops and wanted the bear dead.

In theory, the bear should have been relatively easy to catch. After all, the bear wore a radio beacon around its neck. Wardens had the bear under electronic surveillance. They loaded up rifles, recruited a posse, and took to the hills in pickup trucks. Pilots flew overhead to track the bear's radio signal and relay the bear's whereabouts to officials on the ground. But the North Fork is tremendously thick and rugged country. The bear was constantly on the move. Wardens were always one step behind the Giefer bear. Then they would receive another irate phone call: The bear had trashed yet another cabin. It was difficult to keep track, but authorities figured the bear broke into cabins fifty-five times. He hit some cabins twice. The bear was making the wardens look like a backwoods version of the Keystone Cops.

"We got him smartened up, and now we hope to trip him up," warden Lornie Diest told a local newspaper reporter. "He's got to make a mistake sometime. He's no ordinary bear. He's so smart one would think he had a doctor's degree."

At one cabin, the bear ripped down the front door but opened the cupboards without a scratch. At another, the bear spilled a bag of flour and tracked white, powdery paw prints on the plywood floor. At a third place, it appeared the bear napped on a cot, like Papa Bear in the children's story.

Trappers, wardens, biologists, and members of the sheriff's posse ground their teeth in frustration. Biologists placed carcasses near cabins and baited them with a special drug designed to give the bear a grizzly-size bellyache. The idea was that the bear would eat the meat, suffer the consequences, and learn to leave cabins alone. The bear ignored the temptation. Steel-jaw bear traps, not used for decades, were dusted off and put back in service. At one point, trappers knew that Giefer lingered in the brush near a baited trap site for more than two hours, juggling his caution and his appetite. Yet Giefer never took the bait.

"Without a trace of remorse, he is a go-to-hell, shaggy, bad-ass bruin in the best tradition," wrote North Fork author Douglas Chadwick. Folks up the North Fork started keeping loaded rifles within easy reach. Chadwick compared the bruin to infamous outlaws like Jesse James or Butch Cassidy. "Which of them, and who among us, could so long and successfully wage lawlessness in the face of space-age technology—with a beacon sealed around his neck?"

Things were going badly enough for the bear's pursuers when they received another stroke of bad luck. The bear ripped into a cabin and caught his radio collar on a nail. The snagged collar slipped off the bear's head and was found by the cabin owner. With no way to track the bear's movements, the wardens could only follow the trail of one ruined cabin after another.

Federal wildlife agents blew into town in a new pickup truck. Wedum remembers them as cocky—bragging that they would soon bring Giefer to justice. Sure enough, in late September 1976, the federal trappers caught a big male grizzly in a snare. During the capture they inadvertently gave the bear too much of an immobilizing drug and killed it.

In the 1970s Polebridge was a tiny village of hippies, gyppo loggers, and back-to-the-land types. Hearing of the bear's demise, the Northern Lights Saloon held a wake. The bear had earned begrudging respect, even from those whose homes he had ransacked.

Happy that they had succeeded where local-yokels had failed, the federal agents called the press. A newspaper sent a photographer to take pictures of the carcass. Only then did the federal trappers bother to look at the bear's lip. They were shocked to find no tattoo. They had captured and killed the wrong bear, an innocent bruin protected by federal law. They packed up and returned home, a picture of chagrin.

The Giefer grizzly was still on the lam. "Even the grizzly-haters marveled," Chadwick said. "You got to admit he beat 'em, by God. Beat 'em flat out, beat 'em every whichway, beat 'em at their own game. He plumb snookered those smart government boys. No way around it. That's some goddam bear!"

In October 1976 Giefer went silent. No cabin owners reported any problems for several weeks. It was like the old troublemaker had evaporated.

Rumors started to fly. So-and-so shot old Giefer. Whatshisname saw the carcass himself. Same old story: Shoot, shovel, shut up. Chadwick figured someone had done in the old bear. Ostrom wrote an editorial, urging the shooter to come forth: "If one of you killed the bear, then for cryin' out loud, let the rest of us know one way or another. We won't rat on you... Let's end this tragic-comedy in the most honorable way we can."

Then in November, just as bears prepare for their winter dens, another cabin in the North Fork Valley was busted up. Then another. Someone measured the paw tracks in the snow. They matched Giefer's prints. It was almost hibernation time, but Giefer was still up to his old games. Hit and run. Catch me if you can.

•   •   •

AFTER THE NOVEMBER SNOWS, Giefer retreated to some secret mountain den. It was a light winter, followed by an early spring. With the April thaw, he emerged and began roaming.

For some reason known only to him, he wandered north. He crossed a long, narrow, straight strip of land that had been cleared of trees from east to west. The deforested strip meant nothing to Giefer, but he had crossed the international boundary between the United States and Canada. In Montana, the bear had been a federally protected species. In British Columbia, he was legal game, a trophy rug on legs.

Ray Koontz, a supermarket owner from McConnellsburg, Pennsylvania, arrived in Canada that April with a grizzly bear hunting license. He had killed a smallish grizzly one time before in Alaska, but this time he vowed to hold out for a trophy specimen. He hired a local guide and they packed deep into

the Wigwam River drainage in southeastern British Columbia.
They hunted three days, spending each dawn and dusk
watching the remote meadows that were blushing green with
spring grass. They watched a small, light-colored bear and heard
others in the woods around them. Finally they spotted a big
grizzly bear that Koontz could not pass up.

Koontz stalked the bear until he found himself within range
of his .340-magnum rifle. The first shot to the neck probably
killed the bear, but Kootnz fired twice more for insurance. The
bear was a fine trophy, almost nine feet long from nose-to-tail.
Upon examining the downed bear, Koontz noted metal clips
in the bear's ears. This bear had a police record. It was the
Giefer grizzly.

The Giefer bear had probably garnered more newsprint than
any single bear in Montana history. His story was told in *Sports
Illustrated* and *Reader's Digest*. Now the bear's story was brought
to an abrupt end in three quick rifle shots.

Koontz's guide skinned the bear on the spot. Koontz would
have the bear mounted, life size, on a papier-mache boulder,
snarling and with claws out-stretched.

Montana newspaper reporters called Koontz for interviews.
Ostrom wrote the headline in bold: The Giefer Creek Grizzly
Is Dead.

People of northwestern Montana learned several hard lessons from Giefer. One, backwoods property owners learned it
was wise not to leave tempting trash and other food near cabins. Wildlife managers learned that tolerating bears that break
into cabins is generally a waste of time and can inflame public
opinion against bears. People also garnered a full measure of
respect for the grizzly's stealth, strength, and street smarts.

Ostrom probably encapsulated the community's feelings: "I
felt relief tinged with sadness," he wrote. "Relief because
my property on the Canadian border is now safe from his

raids, but sadness because he was a beautiful and highly intelligent creature....I knew it had to end this way. I feel we were lucky no one was hurt or killed by the bear, but nevertheless am a little sad."

As a flesh-and-blood bear, Giefer is dead and gone. But as a legend, he is as alive as ever.

Nightmare at
Rainbow Point

THE STATES OF MONTANA, IDAHO, AND WYOMING CONVERGE LIKE three pieces of an enormous jigsaw puzzle. Between the crags of the Continental Divide and the glassy waters of the Madison River sits the village of West Yellowstone, Montana. Ever since the village was hewn from the forest, it has been the western gateway to Yellowstone National Park. A collection of gas stations, tackle shops, hotels, restaurants, and bars, the village serves as base camp for sightseers, anglers, horseback riders, and backpackers. West Yellowstone was founded on fun.

On June 24, 1983, Ted Moore and Roger May of Sturgeon Bay, Wisconsin, were two more visitors in the steady stream of tourists that swamp West Yellowstone every summer. The men were several days into their western camping vacation, seeking fun and finding it. Their goal for the night was Hebgen Lake, a picturesque reservoir on the Madison River nine miles northwest of West Yellowstone and five miles from the park boundary.

Moore and May arrived at West Yellowstone and drove north on U.S. Highway 191. A few miles outside of town, they turned onto a Forest Service road. Gravel rattled against their car's undercarriage as they continued down a peninsula above Hebgen Lake. Five miles later they found Rainbow Point Campground, a Forest Service site along the lakeshore. They drove past a sign warning campers that a bear had been in the area. The sign recommended camping only in "hard-sided" campers and trailers. The men pulled into Loop A, selected campsite number 17, and pitched their tent.

The men were prepared to enjoy their vacation to the fullest. They lit up a portable barbecue and put on steaks, corn, and sweet potatoes. The smell of cooking meat wafted through the campground and made the men smile with anticipation. They were grubby after a couple of days of camping, but they didn't mind. After dinner, they meticulously cleaned up after themselves, putting away the food, grill, and cooking utensils.

May and Moore knew enough to keep a clean camp. Although bears were in the area, there hadn't been any bear trouble at the campground that season. They didn't want to make any. Since it was near the summer solstice, the evening stretched long. Gradually, the campground began to fill. But to May and Moore, the campground seemed quiet, even a little dull. So May and Moore got back in their car and drove back to West Yellowstone for a couple of beers. They returned to camp by eleven or so. They crawled into their sleeping bags and fell asleep. Only one of them would live until morning.

•   •   •

THE WARNING SIGN at the campground entrance was a direct response to one particular bear known as No. 15. Before the summer was over, No. 15 would make national news and spark a raging controversy throughout the National Park Service, Montana Fish, Wildlife and Parks, and affiliated agencies.

No. 15 was a big male, the kind of animal that had been the undisputed boss of Yellowstone for thousands of years. He also was a classic example of what newspapers call a "problem bear" or "garbage bear." From the bear's perspective, he was just another animal trying to make a living in the habitat in which he was born. Making a living mostly meant finding food. Around Yellowstone, food comes in a variety of packages. Sometimes, food is an elk carcass in a frozen river or spawning cutthroat trout in a mountain stream. Another time, food may be a cheeseburger and fries tossed out a car window.

No. 15 had a long history as a trash-eater. As an immature bear in 1971, the bruin caught the attention of rangers by eating trash at Pelican Campground in the center of Yellowstone National Park. Between 1971 and 1983, researchers and bear managers caught No. 15 twenty times, or roughly twice a summer. Many grizzly bears wise up to traps after being caught once or twice. Not No. 15. The bear became so familiar with traps that he often stole the bait without getting caught. Even when caught, it seemed the bear figured that capture was fair trade for a free meal.

A trapped bear is often tranquilized so it can be handled safely. Over the years No. 15 had felt the sting of an immobilizing dart at least twelve times. The practice of drugging bears in order to capture them dates back nearly 100 years. In the eastern United States in 1820, an enterprising black bear trapper spiked buckets of honey with strong liquor and fed the concoction to wild bears until they passed out drunk. Since then, the practice has grown more sophisticated, with precise drug dosages measured by the milligram and administered by a dart fired from an air rifle. In the 1970s a drug called Sernylan was a favorite immobilizing drug for its reliable and potent knockdown power. Bear No. 15 had been immobilized with Sernylan six times.

Sernylan was developed as a surgical anesthetic for humans. By 1968 the government banned the drug for medical use because of severe side effects. Pharmaceutical companies repackaged the drug and sold it to veterinarians for tranquilizing animals for surgery. Marketers named the drug Sernylan because it sounded like "serene." But by the late 1970s, even veterinarians dropped Sernylan. The federal government was cracking down on the drug because it was being abused on the streets.

Even if you're not a doctor, veterinarian, or bear-trapper, you've probably heard of Sernylan. Cops know it as PCP, which is short for its chemical name of phencyclidine. On the street, PCP is called "angel dust." According to the U.S. Department of Health, PCP is one of the more notorious hallucinogens. Its well-documented and severe psychological side effects include disorientation, confusion, anxiety, irritability, paranoia and violent behavior. That's in the psyche of a human being. What of a bear? Could a drug that has devastating effects on the human mind also make an animal's brain haywire? Moreover, could the "angel dust" given bear No. 15 have triggered what happened that night at Rainbow Point Campground?

• • •

ABOUT TWO-THIRTY in the morning, May and Moore awoke to find their tent shaking. In his semiconscious haze, Moore thought someone was playing a prank on them. He muttered something to May. The poles shook even more violently until the entire tent collapsed. Then May began screaming.

The bear's first bite caught May in the upper torso. The bear tore a hole in the side of the tent and pulled May into the open. Moore didn't bother finding and unzipping the tent door—he followed his friend out the hole in the tent.

Outside, the moon offered meager light. Only ten feet away, Moore saw a massive animal standing over his screaming friend. Then, quick as a shot, the bear grabbed May's ankle in its jaws and ran off into the darkness, dragging May as if he were a piece of elk.

Moore was stunned at the speed with which the animal had disappeared. Moore looked desperately for some kind of weapon, any tool that would help defend himself and his friend. He found perhaps the flimsiest of any weapons ever used against a grizzly bear—an aluminum tent pole. Moore charged toward his friend's screams. When he saw the bear again, he hurled the pole at the animal like a spear. The tent pole clattered harmlessly to the ground. Still, the bear backed off, leaving May in the dirt.

"Are you all right?" Moore asked.

May's voice returned weakly: "I'm okay...but I'm not doing so good."

Moore realized how utterly helpless he was. He could barely see. He needed a flashlight. He needed his glasses. He could light up the whole campsite with the headlights of the car, if he could only find the keys.

Moore dashed back to camp and rifled through the mass of torn nylon that had been their tent. He spent several frantic moments feeling around for a flashlight. He felt panic rising inside him and fought to restrain it. In the darkness, Roger May began screaming anew. The bear had returned. Moore spun on his heels, staring into the black of the night. Then came a sound even more terrifying: May suddenly went silent.

By now the ruckus had roused other campers. Some arrived with flashlights while others turned on their car headlights. They strained to hear any sound of the missing camper.

The bear remained hidden in the forest, beyond the power of the campers' lights. Someone called the sheriff's office. About three-twenty in the morning, the local sheriff's deputy arrived. The bear picked that moment to drag the corpse of Roger May across the road behind the patrol car.

The sheriff recruited a rescue party, amassing what he hoped would be enough people to keep the bear away. With lights blazing, the rescuers followed the bloody drag marks through the campground. Within ten minutes, they found what was left of Roger May, fifty feet from the campground road and 200 feet from the original attack. About seventy pounds of May's body—roughly one third of his body weight—had been consumed or lost as blood.

• • •

STATE AND FEDERAL WILDLIFE AUTHORITIES DESCENDED upon the scene. Deputies cleared out the campground as wildlife authorities saturated the area with thirteen traps. Within twenty-four hours, they caught Bear No. 15 in a trap ten feet away from slot 17, Loop A. The bear fell for a trap baited with garbage. Rangers found traces of human material in the bear's fecal matter and promptly killed No. 15.

National Park Service bear biologist Kerry Gunther figures the odds of being injured by a bear in Yellowstone National Park is somewhere around one in 2.1 million. The odds of being killed by a grizzly bear are several times smaller than that, and the odds of being injured by a grizzly in a "frontcountry" campground like Rainbow Point even smaller. Most grizzly bear incidents occur in the backcountry.

Between 1975 and 2001, some 60 million people visited Yellowstone National Park and the surrounding area. Only one of those people was harmed by a bear in a developed area. That person was Roger May.

Rangers investigating the attack could find no fault with any of the things May and Moore did. Their camp was flawlessly clean. The only mistake experts could identify was electing to camp in a tent when the campground was posted for hard-sided campers and trailers.

Government wildlife agencies are open targets for public review and criticism. Soon after the death of Roger May, some critics speculated that repeated doses of Sernylan might have triggered No. 15's attack. CBS News launched the idea into the national spotlight in its evening broadcast. The bear attack story was juxtaposed against footage of drug addicts going berserk under the effects of angel dust. Government critics latched onto the hypothesis; they alleged that government biologists were responsible for May's death by turning a peaceable animal into a man-eater. No doubt the allegations were dramatic, even scandalous. But were they true?

* * *

GLACIER NATIONAL PARK Chief Ranger Steve Frye has worked in both Yellowstone and Glacier and knows something of handling bears. Indeed, Frye's father was also a ranger and was the first person to drug grizzly bears in Glacier National Park. Frye firmly doubts that Sernylan made No. 15 some kind of ursine junkie. However, he believes the bear's history with people (including its capture history) may have had other, more subtle effects.

"People love to attribute human characteristics to animals, especially bears," Frye said. "To say that a drug would cause a bear to hallucinate just because it causes hallucinations in humans is anthropomorphism at its best."

More important, Frye says, is the fact that No. 15 had been caught over and over. Yet the bear still actively sought out bait and garbage. No. 15 had learned that humans offered free food, even in traps. Drugs or no drugs, it's dangerous for a bear to associate people with food.

Keith Aune, who heads the Montana Department of Fish, Wildlife and Parks's wildlife laboratory in Bozeman, concurs.

"Part of the problem is we cannot say for certain that Syrnalin was not a factor," Aune said. "But there are big differences between the brains of humans and the brains of most wildlife species, including bears. Syrnalin was used on hundreds and hundreds of animals in zoos and in the wild, without causing any of the side effects or other problems one might suspect.

"The larger question is, was it judicious and proper to capture this bear twenty times? I would say, no, probably not. No bear should be handled twenty times. Most researchers would agree that's excessive, no matter the drug. Three or four times are fine. Six or seven is pushing it. Nineteen or twenty is too much." Today such a bear would be destroyed or sent to a zoo much earlier in its capture history.

But people—and moreover the news media—often latch on to a single, sensational explanation after an attack.

"We want to find simple answers," Aune said. "It's human nature. We want to pin down the problem to a single reason why. People say, that bear had bad teeth. Or they say, that bear was given drugs that made it go crazy. But reality is a lot more complicated. Most of the time, several things are happening at once—a convergence of probabilities. It's never one simple cause."

In Yellowstone, garbage and bears go back to 1872, when the park was founded for its collection of geysers and hotpots. By the 1890s, scores of bears frequented the hotel garbage pits and became fearless of humans. Bears became one of the tourist attractions at Yellowstone, both mooching from the roadside and feeding in dumps. Bleachers were erected at dumps so tourists could watch the show. Sometimes visitors watched fifty bears at once, chowing down on garbage. Begging bears—particularly black bears—were dangerous. One Yellowstone ranger station recorded eighty-eight visitors bit or scratched by black bears in September 1924. That's nearly three injuries per day!

Starting in 1959, biologists Frank and John Craighead began to study Yellowstone's grizzly bear ecology. They found that garbage dumps, including the one at West Yellowstone, had become major food sources for the park's bears. At the largest Yellowstone dump, a spot called Trout Creek, the Craigheads sometimes counted eighty grizzly bears *at once*. The Craigheads compared the dumps to the congregations of bears at salmon spawning streams such as Alaska's McNeil River, which also attracts scores of bears at a time. The Craigheads pointed out there is nothing particularly new about bears cleaning up human garbage. For example, over thousands of years grizzlies probably congregated at buffalo jumps to dine on bison parts left behind by Indians. To a bear's view, modern garbage dumps were no different.

But times were different in the 1960s. National Park Service managers were weary of dealing with bears that were hooked on garbage. Garbage-spoiled bears sometimes became destructive or dangerous. In Yellowstone's Thoroughfare region, grizzlies seeking food demolished a backcountry cabin so many times that rangers eventually gave up rebuilding it. Then in 1967, two young women were killed by garbage-eating grizzlies in Glacier National Park. The entire National Park Service was under tremendous political pressure not to have a repeat incident in Yellowstone.

As part of the solution, the National Park Service wanted bears to return to more natural diets, and the sooner the better. In 1970 the National Park Service closed the dumps and hauled park garbage to landfills outside the park. But bears are resourceful. There was still garbage around. The bears just had to look harder for it.

Bear No. 15 was first caught at Yellowstone's Pelican Campground in 1971, the year after the Yellowstone dumps were closed. Rangers hauled him to the backcountry and let him go.

As No. 15 grew older, garbage gradually became a larger part of his diet. In 1974, No. 15 was captured three times at the West Yellowstone town dump, just outside the park. Up until 1982, No. 15 fed on trash intermittently. That autumn, he seemed to focus more on trash and less on natural foods. In biologists' jargon, No. 15 was "food-conditioned" in that he associated people with a free lunch. But he was not particularly aggressive. Every time rangers pressed the bear, he ran off.

After No. 15 killed May in 1983, investigators found "strong evidence" that the bear ate garbage or dog food from homes near Rainbow Point Campground. Experts do not know exactly what pushed No. 15 to the point it decided to rip through a tent to kill and eat Roger May. But it's a safe bet his long history of eating human garbage was the major factor in the attack.

As Stephen Herrero wrote: "Number 15 wasn't an overly aggressive bear. It was a bear that had learned over many years that people and garbage, or trap sites, yielded food. Number 15 had lost some of its fear of people and in the quiet of a sleeping camp, this lack of fear combined with unknown other factors, and Roger May was attacked and killed."

That reality of No. 15 and Roger May is a lot less sensational than a story about a drug-crazed bear.

Lenny, The Bulletproof Bear

Wayne Kasworm knelt in the wet snow, cold moisture seeping through the knee of his pants. He looked closely at the dark splatter in the snow and then touched it with a fingertip. Given his circumstances, it was about the worst thing he could find.

Kasworm was a field biologist working for the Montana Department of Fish, Wildlife and Parks, but on that late November day in 1984, he was something of a backwoods detective. The splatter was blood. There was a wounded grizzly in the forest. Kasworm knew that much when he stepped into this assignment. The blood told him more. The blood reflected a yellowish-brown tint. It was somewhat greasy to the touch.

Blood is an important clue when tracking a wounded animal. An animal shot through the lungs will bleed bright pink blood, frothy with oxygen. That's an indication that the animal is probably fatally wounded and will soon die. Dark red blood indicates a wound to muscle tissue and indicates the animal may or may not be wounded badly. But yellow-brown, greasy blood indicates something else entirely: Gut shot.

Kasworm, fellow biologist Shawn Riley, and game warden Chester Lameroux were in the snowy forest near Trout Creek,

Montana, in the Clark Fork Valley. "Gut shot" were the last words they wanted to say, but that's what the evidence clearly showed. In the wild, gut shot animals generally die, but die slow, agonizing deaths. In the meantime, a wounded grizzly is a notoriously dangerous animal. Kasworm and crew had a thoroughly unenviable job on their hands. Their imaginations churned out potential resolutions to the predicament. None of them were good.

• • •

HERE'S WHAT LANDED THEM in the fix: Thanksgiving was the final weekend of Montana's big game hunting season. Thousands of hunters took the last chance to try to fill their freezers with elk or deer meat. Hunting conditions were excellent around Trout Creek. A storm had dumped ten inches of snow, making for quiet stalking and providing perfect tracking.

One local hunter cut fresh tracks made by a bear—and a big one. The hunter was a little surprised, since most black bears were asleep in their winter dens by now. No matter, the hunter had a black bear license and the black bear season was still open.

Winter temperatures in the Trout Creek area are mild by Montana standards and the forest is lush and thick. Creek bottoms are dominated by western red cedar and side slopes grow dense with alder and grand fir. The hunter followed the bear tracks, rifle at ready, sneaking through the woods. His boot prints followed the paw prints for a quarter of a mile, the tension building with every step.

An experienced tracker can differentiate between the tracks of a black bear and a grizzly bear, but not everyone can. On a grizzly track the claws are longer and the toe pads form a straight line, where a black bear's toes form more of an arc. When snow is deep and soft, those distinctions are difficult to discern. The idea that the tracks might be made by a grizzly bear didn't register with the hunter. The forest near Trout Creek, particularly south of the Clark Fork River, is not commonly thought of as grizzly habitat.

The hunter entered a particularly dense thicket, holding his rifle at ready. The bear had chosen that thicket to sleep away the day. The hunter found himself within a few yards of the bedded bear.

It's not perfectly clear if the bear charged or merely rushed to get away from the hunter. It made little difference. The hunter threw up his rifle and fired. He was about three feet from the bear when he first pulled the trigger. With the shot, the bear stumbled against a tree. The hunter fired again, this time from about nine feet.

"I don't blame the guy for shooting the bear at that point," Kasworm said later. "He was in fear for his life. Most people would have done exactly the same thing."

A .30-06-caliber rifle is a tremendous weapon, capable of killing any land animal in North America. When the bullet flies from the barrel, it moves a half-mile per second and carries a ton and a half of energy. The hunter fired two shots into the bear—three tons of punishing energy at nearly point-blank range—but the bear got back on its feet and kept on running.

Once the hunter had a good look at the bear he realized his mistake. There was no open season on grizzly bears. He turned around, hiked out of the woods, and found a telephone. To his credit, the hunter told wildlife authorities he had wounded a grizzly. Kasworm's plans for the Thanksgiving holiday immediately changed.

•   ▪   •

KASWORM AND FELLOW BEAR RESEARCHER Tim Thier already knew this bear. It was a 400-pound male they had numbered 680.

Thier had nicknamed the bruin Lenny.

Kasworm and Thier were two years into a research project for the state of Montana. Mining companies were interested in extracting minerals from the Cabinet Mountains, a range between Trout Creek and Libby, Montana. Since the Cabinets are grizzly bear habitat and since grizzly bears are listed as a threatened species under the Endangered Species Act, the mining company funded research to learn more about the bears.

Kasworm and Thier set traps in the Cabinet Mountains for nearly two years before they finally caught the 11-year-old male. He was only the second grizzly they had to show for their efforts. They caught plenty of black bears, but with so few grizzlies remaining in the Cabinets, catching one proved very difficult. Thier was so excited when he finally caught a Cabinet Mountains grizzly that he passed out cigars to all his friends.

The researchers found that the Cabinet Mountains grizzly bear population was hanging on by the thinnest thread. They eventually estimated that fewer than fifteen grizzly bears remained in the region. The population was so low, the U.S. Fish and Wildlife Service eventually imported four young female grizzly bears from British Columbia and released them into the Cabinet range to keep the population alive.

Lenny was one of the original Cabinet Mountains grizzlies. After fitting Lenny with a radio-collar and turning him loose, researchers soon learned Lenny was a wandering bear with a home range of 800 square miles. He left the Cabinets and roamed twenty miles to the south, swimming the Clark Fork River and dashing across U.S. Highway 200. The bear roamed a mountainous strip between the Clark Fork River and the Idaho border. In the fall of 1984, Lenny was probably scavenging gut-piles from deer and elk killed by hunters.

•   ▪   •

WHEN KASWORM'S TEAM investigated the shooting scene, they studied the clues left in the snow and the signals from Lenny's radio collar. The evidence on the ground confirmed the hunter's story.

They followed the bear's tracks. The print from the right forepaw was full of blood, indicating the animal had been hit in the shoulder, as they suspected. But worse, there were splashes of yellow-brown fluid in the snow. The trackers took that to be fluid from the stomach or intestines. They followed the bear for about a third of a mile. The bear laid down eleven times but always got up and resumed moving.

The trackers figured the bear would die. They just worried how long the animal would suffer and if he would put anyone in danger. Lameroux argued they should track down the bear and kill it. Leaving the bear to suffer was unnecessary for the bear and could endanger people, he argued.

Kasworm held an antenna in one hand and a radio receiver in the other. The steady beeps told him Lenny was still alive.

As soon as they learned about the wounded bear, authorities closed the forest to the public. Thanksgiving weekend marked the end of the hunting season anyway. People would be leaving the mountains for the winter. If Lenny didn't die first, he would soon hibernate. The bear moved into forest above the town of Noxon. The crew decided to leave the bear alone, since it seemed unlikely the bear was going to hurt anyone.

The bear's prognosis was grim. Generally a gut wound doesn't cause an animal to bleed to death. The real problem is peritonitis (the acute inflammation of the abdominal cavity) and accompanying bacterial infection. In a ruptured, traumatized intestine, dangerous bacteria grow out of control, producing toxins that invade the animal's blood stream. These toxins eventually cause the heart to fail or the animal to go into extreme shock. At best, death can take hours. More likely it will drag on for days. People who have suffered peritonitis report that the pain is agonizing.

"We decided to stand back and let nature take its course," Kasworm said. "Animals wounded in that sort of way really don't stand much of a chance of survival at all."

· · ·

On November 25, Tim Thier hauled a camper-trailer to a place where he could receive the signal from Lenny's radio collar. He camped out, listening to the signal that told him the bear was still moving. On December 4, another storm blew in and the bear finally settled in for the winter.

When winter comes to Montana, most grizzly bears climb to remote high country where they excavate an underground hibernation chamber. Lenny evidently didn't have the strength for that. He remained at a relatively low elevation, scooped out a cavity on the top of a rotten stump, added a few fir boughs for a bed, and fell asleep. He simply allowed the falling snow to bury him.

Over the winter, Kasworm occasionally flew over the Clark Fork Valley. Lenny's signal remained strong. The radio had a special motion sensor so if the bear died and stopped all movement the radio would send out a special signal. That signal never came. All winter long, Lenny would occasionally shift in his sleep, letting Kasworm know he was still alive.

Spring came and Lenny emerged into the sunshine through a layer of snow. He descended into the low country, looking for green grass, winter-killed elk, or anything else he might eat. Lenny wandered north, back across Highway 200, and swam the Clark Fork River. When he returned to the Cabinet Mountains, Kasworm and Thier were waiting for him.

In May 1985, they set a series of baited snares in Lenny's home range. Lenny took the bait. Once again, the bear was in hand. After being shot twice and overwintering in a sorry excuse for a den, what condition would Lenny be in?

Using an air gun, Thier thumped Lenny with a tranquilizing dart and Lenny slumped asleep. Kasworm and Thier had about an hour to work before the drug wore off. The biologists first replaced Lenny's collar. (That's always the first step in these operations; if the bear somehow shrugs off the drugs, researchers can abandon the rest of the job and still keep tabs on the bear.)

At first glance, Lenny appeared just fine. His coat was glossy and thick. The men took out a tape measure and measured the bear's girth. A mathematical formula allowed them to estimate the bear's weight. To their surprise, his weight was normal. In fact, Lenny had gained perhaps forty pounds since the summer before.

Then the men began probing the bear's fur. Near the right shoulder they found two bullet holes: One small entry hole and one larger, more ragged exit wound. A chunk of bone was sticking out of the exit wound. Thier used dental instruments to extract the fragment—a piece of shoulder blade about the size of a silver dollar. One bullet had evidently struck the shoulder blade and deflected off, taking a chunk of bone with it. The trappers removed the piece of bone and cleaned the wound as best they could with a dose of disinfectant.

Knowing the bear had also been shot in the right side of the abdomen, Thier examined the bear the bear's right flank. He found nothing, so they rolled the bear over.

Thier found a second wound, again only partially healed. This wound was almost dead center in the bear, toward the rear of the ribcage. This time, it was the exit wound. Just under the hide, Thier saw something shiny: It was what was left of the bullet, still lodged in the bear. Gently, Thier removed the slug. Part of the bullet had broken off and exited the bear's body, but a larger chunk of lead remained inside the bear, lodged under the bear's thick, elastic hide.

Thier and Kasworm were simply dumbfounded. There was no gangrene, no maggots, no bad smell or pus around any of the wounds. Neither wound appeared to be the least bit infected. They were particularly amazed by the second wound: The bullet evidently passed completely through the bear near the rear of the ribcage, which houses the liver, lungs, and other vital organs.

"You tell me how that bullet could have passed through there without hitting something vital," Thier said, shaking his head years later. "The bullet must have traveled completely through the bear's body. It's almost inconceivable that this bullet bypassed what would normally be considered vital organs."

Kasworm and Thier trimmed and cleaned the wounds and then backed off. Lenny roused from the drug and shuffled off into the mountains.

•   ▪   ◦

IN RETROSPECT, Kasworm can explain how Lenny survived wounds that would kill lesser animals. For one thing, Lenny went into hibernation only days after being shot. For the next five months he ate nothing. That means no food or digestive fluids interfered with his damaged intestines, giving them an opportunity to heal.

For another, bears live rough-and-tumble lives in a rough-and-tumble world. A bear's skeletal structure and musculature can withstand amazing punishment. And finally, natural selection has endowed bears with a remarkably effective immune system. This makes sense, since bears are scavengers who spend much of their time in highly septic situations such as feeding on rotten carcasses. Adult males frequently wear jagged scars on their faces from being lain open by the dirty claws of rival bears. Yet for all these injuries, researchers and hunters who handle bears report that the animals rarely show infections. Bears prone to infection were weeded out of the gene pool many generations ago.

Thier recalls another grizzly bear that recovered from daunting injuries. In 1988, while trapping in the South Fork of the Flathead River, researchers caught a young male grizzly that had a gaping, fist-size wound in its rear leg. Evidently another, more dominant male had bitten the younger animal in the rump, tearing out a piece of muscle that Thier estimated weighed as much as three pounds. But that wasn't all. The young bear had been in an earlier fight in which a bigger bear had bitten the smaller animal in the face. That bite blinded the young bear in one eye and a fang punctured its snout near that eye. When the bear exhaled, air exited the puncture wound as if it were a third nostril. Yet the wound healed. Researchers nicknamed him Popeye.

Later, Popeye was killed by a hunter and Thier examined the hide and skull. He found the bear's rump injury had healed completely. The skull showed a fracture line deep across its snout. "The bigger bear had darned near ripped his face off," Thier said.

* * *

LIKE LAZARUS, Lenny was once again among the living. Thier and Kasworm resumed their monitoring, following Lenny from truck and airplane. For the rest of 1985, Lenny roamed broadly throughout his usual home range. If anything, Lenny traveled even more widely than he had the previous year. During the mating season, he courted a local female.

That fall, Lenny once again left the Cabinet Range, crossed the Clark Fork and returned to the mountains near Trout Creek. In December 1985, Lenny's radio collar began sending the signal that indicated the collar hadn't moved. Kasworm flew over the area and pinpointed the signal in a basin in Idaho, just over the state border.

It was late fall and once again hunting season was under way. Kasworm feared that Lenny may have run afoul of another hunter and this time ended up dead. After the hunting season, Kasworm and another biologist rode snowmobiles into the high country, following the radio signal.

Just over the Bitterroot Divide, Kasworm continued his quest on snowshoes, using a hand-held antenna to track Lenny's signal. The signal led him straight to the intact collar. There was no evidence of foul play. The collar had simply slipped over Lenny's head.

From then on, Kasworm could not keep exact tabs on Lenny. His future trapping efforts failed to recapture the bear. But in the summer of 1986, another biologist spotted a big, lone bear feeding on huckleberries at a high lake in the Cabinet Mountains Wilderness. Kasworm confirmed the color of the ear tags. It was Lenny.

After that, who knows? If Lenny stayed out of trouble, he should have had ten or more years ahead of him. One can only assume Lenny spent the rest of his days afoot in the rugged forests between the Cabinet Range and the Idaho line. Perhaps he is still out there, roaming free in a beautiful and dangerous world.

Death Approaching
Through the Camera Lens

ANY OTHER NIGHT OF THE YEAR, THE SCENE WOULD HAVE BEEN picturesque or even cozy. But not that lonely night in 1987.

It was after midnight in the backcountry of Glacier National Park. Ranger Charlie Logan opened the brass padlock to a backcountry cabin. Inside, he found a Coleman lantern, pressurized the fuel tank, and lit the mantles ablaze. He took the hissing lantern by the bail and perched it next to the cabin window so the light would glow outside. Aside from the stars overhead, it was the only light for miles.

The cabin sat at the base of Elk Mountain alongside an old fire-lookout supply route. Dawn was hours away, but Logan was in no mood for sleep. He stepped outside and shouted into the silent wilderness. His voice faded. The temperature was mild, but a chill seemed to seep up from the very ground.

Finally, about three-thirty in the morning, Logan drew his service revolver. It was a .44 magnum, among the most powerful handguns manufactured. He thumbed back the hammer, pointed the gun toward the ground, and pulled the trigger. Orange flame spat in the dark. The blast shattered the calm night and carried far into the distance. He pulled the trigger once more and the gun fired a second time.

Logan holstered the gun and listened. Logan hoped for a

response—a shout, a gunshot, anything—but heard nothing. Silence was the sound of trouble.

* * *

ELK MOUNTAIN IS A MASSIVE LINEBACKER of a peak near the Continental Divide in southernmost Glacier National Park. Centuries of frigid wind, thin soils, and forest fires have left its shoulders exposed right down to the rock. The scraps of an old fire lookout—rusted metal and shards of glass—litter its 7,835-foot summit. From the lookout, old-time smokewatchers gazed over the Middle Fork of the Flathead and the Badger-Two Medicine country. Everything one can see is grizzly country.

It's a harsh land where snow can drift many meters deep, but scouring winds rarely allow much snow to accumulate on Elk Mountain. The mountain's angle toward the sun ensures that winter snows melt relatively early. The sunlight also triggers spring's first blush of forbs, sedges, and wildflowers on the mountain's flank.

The trail up Elk Mountain is a good early season hike because it is among the first trails in Glacier to melt out. Because of the early green-up, Elk Mountain is also prime spring habitat for grizzly bears. On April 25, 1987, that combination proved big trouble for Charles Wayne "Chuck" Gibbs.

Chuck Gibbs and his wife, Glenda, lived in Libby, Montana, a sawmill town four hours west of Elk Mountain on U.S. Highway 2. They had moved to Montana from North Carolina. She taught first grade while he drove a school bus. Their careers left their summers open to enjoy Montana's wilderness. In particular, Gibbs' passion for wilderness was expressed through his photography. Through talent and dedication, he had amassed files of impressive wildlife shots.

The Gibbs lived near the Cabinet Mountains Wilderness but drove to Glacier at any opportunity. Gibbs considered himself blessed to live in a state that still had enough wilderness to support what he considered the grandest animal of North America, the grizzly bear. He hoped that, in some small way, his photography would help people appreciate and protect the wilderness and all of its inhabitants.

Like hundreds of other wildlife photographers, Gibbs was trying to spin his hobby into a paying proposition. Few animals electrify a photographer's portfolio like a grizzly bear. He had a collection of striking photographs—a black bear up a tree, a regal bull elk standing guard over a harem of cows. But no grizzly bears.

Glenda and Chuck had driven to Glacier for the weekend in their pickup-camper rig. Glenda was still a bit sore from some recent surgery, so she was taking it easy. They stopped at a mineral lick near Essex, where Gibbs stalked a herd of goats in order to take their portraits. Before the day was out, Gibbs also spied a herd of elk and a band of bighorn rams. At the end of that first evening, they found a campsite along a road and slept in their camper. It had been a memorable day.

The second day, Glenda was feeling well enough for a moderate hike. Shortly before noon, they selected the Ole Creek Trail, which skirts the bottom of Elk Mountain. Much of the trail was soft and wet in the spring thaw and the creeks were gushing with meltwater. Grass sprouted where the snow was bare, along with the season's first glacier lilies, yellow fritillaries, and shooting stars. A seasoned woodsman like Gibbs recognized such plants for what they are: spring bear food.

*   *   *

GIBBS WAS NOT EXACTLY OBSESSED with bears but was perhaps fixated on them. His ball cap had a grizzly bear on it and the word, "Montana!" Gibbs carried a Canon single lens reflex camera and a 400-millimeter lens—the workhorse lens of wildlife shooters. Such a lens has the magnifying power of 8X binoculars. It's larger than a man's forearm, fragile, and generally must be used with a tripod. In spite of these inconveniences, such a lens allows one to photograph animals from a distance, even potentially dangerous animals like grizzly bears. In a holster under his arm, Gibbs carried one more piece of equipment, albeit in violation of federal law in a national park: A .45-caliber semiautomatic Colt pistol.

Glenda and Chuck took the hike easy. They paused often, once to chill a can of soda in a snowbank. When streams were too wide for Glenda to cross, Chuck picked her up in his arms and carried her over the water.

Chuck saw the bears first, pointed them out, and handed the binoculars to Glenda. The bears were so far up the mountainside that she didn't at first notice the female grizzly had cubs in tow. She counted three small brown spots behind the larger brown spot. Four grizzlies! A female with three cubs! Less than one-quarter of grizzly litters are triplets. They had never seen such a thing.

"The Lord has been good to me," Chuck Gibbs told his wife, "to let me see so many grizzlies in my life."

They watched the bears for some time before resuming their hike.

"What would you do if that mother bear came after you?" Glenda asked.

"I would try to climb a tree," Chuck said.

The trail took them to a place where they were almost directly below the bears. The female bear rested in the shade of a tree; the cubs clowned around beside her. The mountainside was fairly open. Chuck stopped and looked up the slope.

"I think I'll just go up through this brush and see if I can maybe get some good bear photos," Chuck said, almost casually. He suggested Glenda continue down the trail without him while he approached the bears. He would meet Glenda at the pickup truck at dusk. He made the proposal as if the idea had just popped into his head, although Glenda suspected he had been plotting it ever since he first spied the bears.

* * *

GLACIER PARK RANGER CHARLIE LOGAN was enjoying his evening at the Walton Ranger Station alongside U.S. Highway 2 near the town of Essex. Few people visited this station, particularly in early spring. Logan didn't mind the quiet. He had come to Glacier from Colorado's busy Rocky Mountain National Park and appreciated the solitude. It was a beautiful spring evening and the sun didn't even set until ten o'clock. At ten-thirty, he heard a knock on his door.

He opened the door to Glenda, who introduced herself and immediately said she was worried because her husband was overdue from a hike. She had waited until dark, then come to the ranger station. Overdue hikers are as common as bee-stings. Logan pulled out the standard questionnaire and began asking Glenda a list of questions.

Glenda told Logan that her husband was a skilled outdoorsman but wasn't carrying survival gear. He took medication twice a day for a heart condition. She told him he was carrying a pistol. Moreover, when she last saw him, Chuck Gibbs was stalking a sow grizzly with three cubs with his camera.

Logan suddenly knew this was not a standard search.

* * *

GLENDA'S STORY brought to mind another national park tragedy just several months earlier. That was the story of William J. Tesinsky of Great Falls, Montana. Like Gibbs, Tesinsky was a talented photographer with a knack for capturing good portraits of wild animals. Like Gibbs, Tesinsky was lacking—

and desperately wanted—good images of a grizzly bear.

In the fall of 1986, seven months before Glenda Gibbs knocked on Logan's ranger station door, Tesinsky visited Yellowstone National Park and happened upon bear No. 59— a female grizzly that showed little fear of humans. Yellowstone rangers had already moved that bear five times before Tesinsky saw her near the banks of the Yellowstone River. Tesinsky had borrowed a 1,000-millimeter lens but left the enormous glass in his car when he saw No. 59. Instead, he selected an 80-200 millimeter telephoto zoom. To fill the frame with that lens, he would need to edge his way very close to the bear.

That's exactly what Tesinsky did. Snapping photos along the way, he approached the bear with his camera and tripod. Eventually the bear grew weary of this photographer and lashed out, killing him. Suffering the chronic, pre-hibernation hunger of autumn, the bear ate much of Tesinsky. Rangers investigating the attack scene found Tesinsky's camera, still on the tripod. By studying the camera settings, they estimated Tesinsky was just a few feet from the bear before she finally attacked.

The Yellowstone case was an object lesson for rangers like Charlie Logan—just one more example of what can go wrong when park visitors and wildlife get too close. The story made newspapers and broadcast reports across the United States and topped every media source in Montana. No doubt, Chuck Gibbs had read the news accounts with interest.

* * *

CANADIAN SCIENTIST STEPHEN HERRERO, perhaps North America's foremost authority on bear attacks, discourages people from photographing bears altogether. He argues the practice is dangerous for people and unnecessarily harasses and endangers the animal. The closest range Herrero recommends approaching a bear for a photo is 1,000 feet—about one-fifth of a mile. Mention that to any professional bear photographer and the photographer may very well laugh in your face.

Few businesses are as competitive as nature photography, especially wildlife photography. Overhead—film, camera equipment, travel—is high and profit margins are razor thin if they exist at all. If you want to catch the attention of jaded photo editors, your slides must be sharp and your subject must fill the frame. Even with all the expensive, bug-eyed lenses on the market, getting great images of grizzly bears demands getting close.

There are two ways of getting close. The most common way is easy but expensive: Simply shoot your bears at a game farm or a zoo. Several menageries (including some in Montana) provide well-trained, well-groomed animal models, rented at a handsome day rate. Most commercial grizzly photos are made this way, particularly those ultra-close portraits of snarling bears.

But canned settings have shortcomings. For one, they're expensive for the photographer. Secondly, to a discerning eye, captive bears look phony. They tend to be overweight and develop unnatural bald spots where they rub their cages. For authentic images, there's no match for wild bears. Besides, people like Chuck Gibbs are drawn to wild life photography because the subjects and surroundings are wild. They don't want to take pictures in some damn zoo.

Stalking a wild animal is an ancient thrill, yet a hunter and a photographer stalk in fundamentally different ways. When a predator stalks, the idea is to remain hidden while creeping as close as necessary to pounce or shoot. Photographers favor a different tactic, which has nothing to do with surprise. Photographers wish to avoid startling their subject. They approach the animal gradually but in the open. This demands substantial patience and no small degree of skill at reading an animal's body language. Ideally the photographer approaches so gradually that the animal decides the photographer is not a threat and tolerates or ignores his presence. Wildlife photography is most effective in national parks, where animals are not hunted and where their natural fear of humans is tempered by regular, harmless contact with people.

•   •   •

As Chuck approached the bears, Glenda walked alone. She continued for about an hour and arrived at their camper about six that evening. At eight-thirty, the evening turned to dusk and she expected Chuck any moment. At nine o'clock it was far too dark to take pictures, but there was still no sign of Gibbs. At ten, Glenda could barely contain her nerves. She forced herself to wait fifteen additional minutes. At ten-fifteen she started the truck, drove to Walton Ranger Station, and found Charlie Logan.

After interviewing Glenda, Logan called headquarters and spoke to his boss. They decided Logan should hike to the remote field cabin that night while his boss organized a search party at West Glacier. Logan and Glenda returned to the trailhead. Logan loaned Glenda a park service radio and left her alone in the camper. He then hiked in the dark to the cabin, lit the lantern, and fired his pistol. His signals went unanswered.

By this time, it was only a couple hours to daylight. Logan didn't bother sleeping. He simply waited.

At dawn, Logan began his search solo. With a mother grizzly in the area and a lost, perhaps injured, hiker in the woods, he was on high alert. On the trail, he found the footprints of Glenda and Chuck, even the spot where they split off and Chuck took after the bears and Glenda returned alone. Logan climbed a short ways up the hill and found bear sign, including snowfields where cubs had frolicked. He knew this was the spot to start the search.

Over the course of the day, searchers arrived on the scene from the park, the Flathead County Sheriff's Office, and search-and-rescue teams. A search dog team arrived, as did a helicopter crew from Malmstrom Air Force Base at Great Falls. Logan traced a likely search zone on a topographic map and the crews began combing Elk Mountain.

Members of the search team spread across the mountain, keeping within sight of each other, shouting back and forth. Shortly after three that afternoon—nearly twenty-four hours after Glenda and Chuck Gibbs had split up—Logan's radio crackled with word that Gibbs had been spotted. The searcher who spotted Gibbs called for reinforcements with shotguns and they approached Gibb's motionless form. A few minutes later, a second radio message to Logan confirmed that Gibbs was dead.

Logan hustled to the attack site. While another ranger stayed with Glenda, a helicopter pilot dropped a body bag to the searchers. They carried Gibbs' body to a makeshift-landing zone where the helicopter picked it up.

Logan stayed on the scene with a small crew. The search was now an investigation. They were looking for clues. Before the afternoon was out, they found a most important piece of evidence: Gibbs' camera and a roll of exposed film. That was a piece of good news on an otherwise grim day. The film would help tell Gibbs' final story.

•　•　•

CHUCK GIBBS KNEW a good photo subject when he saw one. The bears were beautiful specimens. The mountain wind rippled their thick fur.

After Gibbs left his wife about five o'clock, he climbed about

1,500 feet up the slope of Elk Mountain. He carried his Canon T-90 camera and telephoto lens in his hands and a gray camera bag slung over his shoulder.

Chuck advanced gradually but intently. His rubber-soled boots felt their way across loose scree and boulders. A passenger train passed on the railroad far below. Gibbs snapped a frame of it, just for kicks.

He had plenty of daylight to work with. At first, he simply wanted to cut the distance between the bears and himself. He needed to approach quickly, but not so quickly that he would panic the bears. The closer he got, the more slowly he moved.

When he approached the bears for the first time, Gibbs left the camera bag on the ground. He didn't want anything slowing him down. He found the bears in his viewfinder, adjusted the light meter, and turned the focus ring to "infinity." The image was sharp. The shutter snapped. At long last, Gibbs had his grizzly shot.

But it wasn't quite enough. He was nearly a hundred yards from the bears. He believed he could do better. He wanted to get closer. He was about 200 feet downhill from them. They moved across the slope above him and he followed from below, firing off frames as the camera's motor drive fed film past the shutter. In a matter of minutes he had taken twenty-four frames.

When a family of bears feeds or travels, they tend to spread out, each following its own nose. But with one warning *huff* from the mother, the cubs will close ranks, staying tight to her side. The mother wants to know where each one is at an instant.

One scientific study found that grizzly bear mothers will "react" to a human within 150 yards. "React" can mean the mother bear will lift her head for a better look or smell. It can mean she will run for the nearest ridge. It can mean she will charge. This female grizzly signaled her cubs to stay close and the three cubs bunched tight to her flanks as Gibbs crept closer. Gibbs didn't mind: He could fit all four bears in one frame that way.

The bears moved off, not breaking into a run but moving out of photographic range. Gibbs alternately picked up his pace and slowed down, trying to keep the bears in camera range without frightening them away. He wanted to capture the bear's faces, particularly their eyes—the key to a good photograph. Every now and then, the female would glance over her shoulder, glaring at Gibbs long enough for him to focus and shoot. At one point, the sow stood up for a better look at Gibbs. He could see her long claws as he tripped the shutter.

As the evening grew late, the light grew richer. Gibbs burned through his first roll of Kodachrome, the motor drive rewinding with a mechanical whine. He popped open the camera to reload. The shots were damned good and Gibbs knew it.

The bears walked in a semicircle around him. His next few shots were getting a bit too far—nearly 300 feet. But then the bears started approaching Gibbs. Without Gibbs advancing at all, the bears cut the distance in half. Gibbs kept on shooting.

There was a line drawn on Elk Mountain the day Chuck Gibbs stalked the four bears. It was an invisible line between the photographer and the bear, and only the mother bear knew exactly where it was. Gibbs may have known it was there, but he didn't know he had crossed it until it was too late.

The bear's ancestors over millions of years had defended cubs from far more formidable beasts than this cameraman. They had survived dire wolves, saber-toothed cats, even giant short-faced bears. Now the sow did what her genetic background told her to do when she and her cubs were threatened: attack and demobilize the threat.

The last frame of Gibbs' camera captured the bears rushing fast toward the intruder. The female is about 170 feet away and running full bore. Even on rough ground a bear can easily run thirty miles per hour, covering about forty-four feet in one second. An Olympic sprinter on a track can cover maybe thirty-three feet a second. Gibbs was no Olympic sprinter and the steep, rocky slope of Elk Mountain was no racetrack. Gibbs moved for a tree. The bear struck Gibbs while he was still on the ground.

Somehow Gibbs still made it to the tree. The injured man scrambled up the trunk, ripping flakes of bark in his desperate climb. Gibbs stretched for the safety of the high limbs, willing himself skyward.

The myth that adult grizzly bears cannot climb trees is an old one that has been written down and passed along since the journals of Lewis and Clark. Like most dangerous myths, there is a grain of truth to it. Unlike black bears, grizzlies are not built for climbing and are not particularly good at it. But given the right tree—and the right motivation—grizzlies can indeed climb. Judging from the torn bark and blood on the trunk of the pine, Gibbs climbed eighteen feet—roughly as high as a second-story window—before the bear caught him. Her sweeping forepaws with those long claws tore Gibbs out of the tree and sent him sprawling to the ground. She attacked him again. Blood loss was extensive.

*　*　*

AFTER THE HELICOPTER DISAPPEARED with Gibbs' body, Logan and the investigators scanned the slope of Elk Mountain for clues. They found Gibbs' ball cap, his Swiss Army knife, and a roll of film. Another object was Gibbs' .45-caliber pistol—outside the holster, the safety in the "fire" position, the gun cocked on a loaded chamber. Logan returned to the scene with a metal detector to try to find any spent cartridge casings. He could not. Eventually Logan determined that Gibbs never had time to shoot.

There was no question what had happened. Gibbs had stalked the bear and pressed her sense of security until she charged to defend her cubs. Gibbs' hobby included a measure of risk and he was caught. The remaining question was, what of the four bears?

The previous autumn, national park rangers in Yellowstone faced a similar decision about what to do with No. 59, the female grizzly that killed Tesinsky. Rangers are sworn to protect park wildlife, and grizzly bears are a federally protected species. Moreover, breeding-age females are particularly valuable in the population. They are not to be wasted wantonly.

In Yellowstone, rangers decided to destroy No. 59. Over years of close contact, No. 59 had lost her fear of people. This lured people to her. Although she might not ever kill another person, the park service was unwilling to risk a repeat attack and the lawsuits that would most certainly follow. Rangers shot No. 59 while she was feeding on Tesinsky's corpse.

Glacier National Park rangers could have followed suit with the bear that killed Gibbs. Using the photographs, a helicopter, and high-powered rifles, they probably could have hunted down the distinctive sow with triplet cubs.

Glenda Gibbs strongly believed the bear should live. Chuck accepted whatever risks came with being in grizzly country and would not want the bear to pay for his errors in judgment. In the end, rangers agreed.

"The decision on how to handle a bear is based on individual bear behavior," Logan said. "It's done on a case-by-case basis. You really can't make any broad generalizations. Mr. Gibbs was encroaching on the bear's territory. He had elected to put himself in that situation."

Logan notes there were important differences between the bear that killed Gibbs in Glacier and the one that killed Tesinsky in Yellowstone. One, Yellowstone's No. 59 had already been moved five times and had a history of trouble with people. No. 59 was so bold she broke into cabins to obtain food. At one point, a cabin owner blasted her in the face with a fire extinguisher. Furthermore, No. 59 ate Tesinsky after killing him. Biology aside, leaving No. 59 would have been a legal liability and a public relations fiasco for the park service.

The Elk Mountain bear was different. She had no known interactions with people. She killed Gibbs simply because she saw him as a threat to her young. She did not eat him. She had acted naturally, as grizzly bears have done for uncounted centuries. Bears will be bears.

Chuck Gibbs—like many of us—was drawn to the grizzly bear in part because it is a powerful, independent creature. He was drawn to the wilderness by the lure of adventure, and adventure, by definition, entails an element of risk. Gibbs would not want the bear dead any more than he would want her wilderness home to be bulldozed and paved. The grizzly and her cubs were allowed to roam free.

Bareback on a Grizzly Bear

🐻

LOU KIS WANTED THE BEAR TO SURVIVE.

In thirty years as a game warden for Montana Department of Fish, Wildlife and Parks, Kis had handled more than 100 grizzly bears. Still, this cantankerous specimen impressed Lou. The bear was coffee-brown from head to toe and tipped 500 pounds at a local truck scale. Its muzzle and face were criss-crossed with scars from territorial battles. One ear was torn off its axis.

Like the scar-faced bear, Lou Kis is something of a scrapper himself. Lou's shoulders, forearms, and wrists have been stout since he was a teenager bucking hay on a Mission Valley farm. As a young man, Kis spent nearly a decade enforcing game laws in the nail-tough mining town of Butte, where hunting and fishing laws were widely considered optional and disputes were sometimes settled with fists. One of Kis's fingers has an unnatural bend to it where he broke it against the jaw of a would-be poacher who had sucker-punched Kis during a routine license check.

"I was ambitious in those days. I wanted to work," Kis said. "There were four things I liked to do: hunting, fishing, catching poachers, and chasing women. And not necessarily in that order."

Humans caused most of Kis's headaches in Butte, but every now and then he had to contend with the occasional black bear. Once, Kis threw a lasso over a black bear that had been spoiled by handouts. The animal shot up a tree as the rope cinched around the bear's midsection. The force threatened to yank Lou up the tree after it. Lou quickly wrapped the rope around the trunk of another tree, halting the bear's escape. Eventually, the bear tired of clutching the tree trunk and Kis finagled the bear into a cage.

"That was the first and last bear I ever roped," Kis recalled. "Everything was a learning process. There were no policies for this kind of thing. The only policy was in your noggin. It was learn-as-you-go."

Eventually, Kis transferred from Butte to Miles City and finally to Kalispell, in the forested mountains of northwestern Montana. This was bear country and Lou's education in bears revved up to full throttle. Kis's beat included thousands of square miles of bear habitat—and a fast-growing population of people.

"Everyone wanted a place in the country. People started moving out into what I call the bears' home, or what the bear considers his home. Most of these people didn't know how to live in bear country. We started having these problems.

"In those days, every little town had a dump. These weren't landfills, they were just dumps. I remember seeing seven or nine grizzly bears at a time at the dump a mile east of Ronan. There was a dump at Essex, another at West Glacier. Pinnacle had a dump. You could see the beat-down bear paths coming into these dumps like spokes on a wheel."

When the bears left the dumps and started raiding garbage cans on rural porches, Kis's telephone rang. Likewise, when a wounded grizzly was seen limping around rural homes, it was Kis's job to investigate. Soon, Kis had a reputation as a bear tracker and bear trapper, hauling his culvert traps from one neighborhood to another and shuttling bears back into the deep woods. One particularly busy autumn, he caught and relocated six grizzlies in eight days.

In 1987 Kis was approaching retirement. By year's end he could leave behind the departmental politics and the late-night telephone calls that accompanied his position as chief regional warden. After decades of baiting bear traps, he looked forward to baiting fishhooks. But fate had one more grizzly waiting.

*   *   *

IN JUNE 1987, time was running out for the scar-faced bear. The bear had roamed the aspen foothills of the Blackfeet Indian Reservation just east of Glacier National Park. The bruin was seen eating a cow on private ranchland. (Which is something different from actually *killing* a cow.) Nonetheless, the former owner of the cow demanded something be done, lest the animal make a habit of eating beef. Federal Animal Damage Control trapper Ken Wheeler caught the scar-faced bear in a cable-snare and darted it with an immobilizing drug.

The usual next step was to ship the bear to a laboratory and destroy it with a lethal injection of drugs. Across the mountains in Kalispell, Kis thought such destruction of a magnificent animal was wasteful. Kis didn't consider snacking on a cow the worst crime a grizzly could commit, especially since there was no hard evidence the bear had actually killed the cow. He told a local newspaper reporter about it: "You know, when you go by the donut shop and you're hungry, what do you do? If it's on your beat you go in and have a donut." So Kis received permission to haul the bear as far from people and cattle as he could and set it free.

Game warden Dave Wedum hauled the scar-faced bear from the Blackfeet Reservation to Kalispell. Wedum has caught more than 400 bears in his career. The scar-faced bear left an impression on Wedum, too.

"I don't think that bear should have ever been turned out in the first place," Wedum recalled. "He was just plain old nasty. He was as bad a bear as I've seen, as far as his disposition goes."

Kis planned to release the bear at Bunker Creek, a tributary of the South Fork of the Flathead River, near the northwestern border of the Bob Marshall Wilderness Area. It's about sixty air miles from the Blackfeet Reservation.

Compared to the Blackfeet Reservation, Bunker Creek looks like a different world. The bear's home range was foothills of grasslands and aspen thickets, backed up against the limestone escarpments of Glacier National Park. Bunker Creek, on the other hand, is a dark, cold-weather jungle of Englemann spruce and subalpine fir. But there were no cattle to tempt the scar-faced bear. To Kis, Bunker Creek seemed the kind of place where a bear might make good on a second chance at freedom.

Kis took possession of the bear in a culvert trap. Most often, culvert traps are welded to a trailer frame and are used to both capture and transport bears. This particular trap was a light-weight aluminum model without wheels or a trailer frame; it was designed to be hauled under a helicopter or in the bed of a pickup. The trap itself weighed 250 pounds—or about half as much as the grizzly inside of it. That day, the trap was in the bed of Kis's government-issue pickup truck. This trap belonged to the federal Animal Damage Control, not Kis's agency, so he was somewhat unfamiliar with it.

Kis and state biologist Shawn Riley had prepared the bear for release by tattooing a number on its lip, bolting a radio-telemetry collar around its neck, and adorning its ear with plastic, numbered tags. Ideally, this apparatus would allow biologists to track the bear should the bear return to cattle country.

So far in 1987, Lou had already released five bears. For him, such releases were routine: Drug the bear, tag it and collar it, and haul it in a culvert trap up a dusty, remote logging road to a spot with plenty of bear food and few people. At the road's end, park the truck and open the trap door. The bear takes a quick look around and darts for the nearest timber.

That's how it goes, almost all of the time. But that's not how it would go that day.

* ● ●

THAT WEEK IN KALISPELL, the Outdoor Writers Association of America was holding its annual conference. One of the authors, Richard Smith of Marquette, Michigan, had written books about black bears and wanted to learn about grizzlies. On Wednesday, July 24, Kis invited Smith and another writer to come along as he released the scar-faced bear. Smith was going to take photographs. FWP biologist Shawn Riley and their local supervisor, Al Elser, joined Smith and Kis. A local U.S. Forest Service ranger, Bert Stout, also came along.

No one knows what goes on in the mind of a grizzly bear when it wakes up in a culvert trap. The bear is in the dark and far from its home. For the first time since it was a tiny cub in a den, the bear cannot move freely about. It may be hungover from the drugs or sick from bouncing about in the back of a pickup truck. Perhaps it feels soreness in its ears, lip, or where it got hit with the tranquilizing dart. It is surrounded by noisy, smelly, dangerous human beings. Any bear in those circumstances is in deep trouble. Perhaps the animal understands something of that.

Before leaving the highway, Kis pulled over at a gas station for sodas. Richard Smith walked around the back of the trap and could smell the bear inside. A deep, menacing growl emerged from the shadowy confines of the trap.

"He made it perfectly clear that he wasn't happy," Smith said. "He wanted people to stay away from him. I got that impression from his growl."

The convoy left U.S. Highway 2 at the town of Hungry Horse, crossed over the Hungry Horse Dam, and drove up the gravel sidewinder of a road that snakes along the bays and inlets of Hungry Horse Reservoir. The jagged profile of Great Northern Mountain rose dramatically to the east, looming over the forest. At the end of the fifty-mile-long reservoir, the road crossed Bunker Creek. Kis led the string of trucks higher into the mountains. Eventually Kis came to a small, wooden bridge over a tributary of Bunker Creek. He stopped. This was the spot.

The bear was riled up, slamming around the inside of the trap, agitated by the long, bouncing ride. The metal can of a trap amplified the bear's noise. Kis took his time to let the bear calm down. He wanted to arrange the scene perfectly for the visiting photographer.

The trap was in the bed of a pickup truck with Shawn Riley at the wheel. His boss, Elser, was literally riding shotgun—in the passenger seat armed with a 12-gauge.

Kis arranged a second pickup truck about 40 yards from the bridge. The Forest Service ranger was driving that rig. Smith scrambled into the bed of the second pickup truck to shoot photographs from there. Kis figured the bear would be thirsty after its confinement and might pause to drink from the nearby creek. If Smith was quick on the shutter, he might have the opportunity for a photo.

Kis instructed drivers in both trucks to keep their motors running while he released the bear. Don't bother setting the emergency brake, he told them. You may have to drive off in a hurry.

From his vantage point in the back of the second pickup, Smith's heart picked up-tempo. This release was routine for

Kis but it was the first grizzly Smith had ever seen. Smith turned the focus ring on his Canon AE1 and thought: *Whatever happens, just keep shooting.*

* * *

OVER THE YEARS, Kis had a few bears turn on him upon release. Once he had to slap a grizzly aside the head with the broadside of an axe to send it on its way. While Kis had plenty of respect for grizzlies, he wasn't afraid of them. He was simply doing a job he had done long enough to become proficient. As a precaution, Kis arranged the holstered .357 magnum revolver on his belt. The gun was loaded in all six chambers.

Kis climbed into the bed of the truck with the trap. To open the trap's door, he had to step on top of the trap and pull the door open. Inside, the bear heard the steps over his head and moved to the front of the trap.

Here's an important detail: The trap was supposed to be chained into the bed of the truck. Someone had forgotten to secure that chain. It would prove to be a disastrous mistake.

Atop the trap, Kis bent down and hoisted the door. He expected the bear to boil out of the trap and dash for cover. At first, the gate wouldn't open. Kis jiggled the door, opening it part way but not enough to free the bear. This infuriated the animal. Finally, Kis yanked the door open and the bear spilled out of the trap.

Kis's troubles only began. As the bear rushed out, it swirled around and began clawing and biting at the metal tube that had robbed it of its freedom. Kis, meanwhile, was still perched on top of the trap.

Kis motioned to Riley to drive off. But Riley didn't see Kis' hand signal. The bear wasn't letting up.

Finally Kis shouted: *"Go! Move the sonofabitch!"*

The instant the bear heard Kis's voice, it turned on the warden.

"The bear reared right up and he got his claws right on top of the trap, right at my feet and he was trying to bite my toes," Kis said. "I pulled my toes back, naturally."

As the bear pressed its forepaws on top of the trap, the truck pulled forward. That sent all hell flying. Like an off-center teeter-totter, the trap tipped out of the pickup truck and crashed to the ground.

The trap, Kis, and the bear were in one thrashing, confused pile. Kis found himself literally on top of the bear.

The bear was momentarily stunned by the thundering load descending upon him. The confusion gave Kis a split second to draw his revolver as man and bear thrashed about in the dust.

"All I know is, I tried to clear leather with my gun. I started pumping lead into his head," Kis said. "It seemed like the thing to do. His head was so damn big I don't know how I could've missed."

He didn't miss. The revolver erupted six times. "I hardly heard that .357 going off," Kis said. "The only noise I heard was when it started clicking on empty."

The first five soft-point bullets ricocheted off the bear's thick skull. Some slugs careened into the bear's body, others into the ground. Meanwhile, the bear knocked Kis down, bit his leg, and began dragging the warden away from the trap.

Kis fired his sixth and final shot from below. The slug smashed through the bear's lower jaw and shattered its spinal column. The bear deflated like a punctured balloon.

"A big bear can kill you in ten seconds flat," Kis said. "No doubt there were a couple other slugs that would have killed the bear, but it probably would have killed me first. That broken neck really sunk him and he went down."

Riley and Elser sprinted toward Kis. They fired more rounds from their shotguns into the still-thrashing bear, making certain it would not get up.

Kis staggered off, shoving the empty revolver back into its holster and picking up his warden's cap. He staggered around and cursed his luck—killing the bear was the last thing he had in mind. Looking down, he noticed his boot filling with blood. Only then did Kis realize he had been hurt. In fact, the bear had sunk its teeth into Kis's right leg a few inches below the knee. The bite snapped his tibia and the bear's teeth had sunk into his fibia. Yet Kis was so charged with adrenaline he walked on the busted leg with no pain.

Kis grew lightheaded and lay down with his foot propped up on a log. Someone radioed for help. The ALERT helicopter ambulance flew in from Kalispell. A squirrelly wind blew in the narrow, timbered canyon, but finally the helicopter was able to set down. Kis didn't particularly want to fly to town— he didn't figure he was hurt that badly—but eventually relented and climbed aboard. Surgeons spent three hours cleaning the four deep punctures (one for each of the bear's two-inch canine teeth) in Kis's leg, setting the broken bone, and bombarding him with antibiotics.

The doctors couldn't cast Kis's leg until they were certain the wounds didn't infect. Kis spent four days in the hospital, his leg in traction. But he healed up and returned to work to finish up until retirement.

*   *   *

BACK IN TOWN, photographer Smith could not believe the near-disaster he had just witnessed. Smith knew the power-winder on his Canon allowed him to shoot five frames a second. He had run through eleven frames in the attack. The whole thing had taken just a few seconds. Smith shipped his film to a processing lab and waited for the results. When the photos arrived at his home in Michigan, Smith had something no other photographer in the world had: A stop-action sequence of life-and-death combat between a man and a grizzly.

"Those photos have been reproduced all over the world," Smith said later. Perhaps the most famous display was a seven-shot sequence in *Outdoor Life* magazine in October 1987.

"My major concern was I didn't want the photographs to reflect negatively on Lou, his agency, or the bear," Smith said later. "Kis was the last person who wanted to kill that bear, but he had no choice under the circumstances."

Likewise, Smith said, the bear was just reacting according to its instincts to a very unnatural situation. In the end, some good did emerge from the snafu, Smith figures. When trapped bears are released today, wardens use a pulley system to hoist the trap door from inside the safety of a pickup cab.

Kis went on to enjoy his retirement, becoming a skilled photographer in his own right. In his den, Kis has a collection of framed photographs and trophy trout on the wall. In the closet, he has a box of "get well" cards he received from all around the country during his convalescence. He also has a collection of clippings from publications from around the world that ran his story and Smith's photos. One tabloid from Australia made up a nearly 100 percent fictional story to go alongside the photos.

One has to wonder why the Australian tabloid bothered to make up anything. The true story is sensational enough.

Grandma Bashes
Bear with Binoculars

"Oh Lord my God, when I in awesome wonder
Consider all the worlds Thy hands have made
I see the stars, I hear the rolling thunder
Thy power throughout the Universe displayed"
Traditional Hymn, *How Great Thou Art.*

WHEN LORRAINE LENGKEEK HIKED THE TRAIL TO ICEBERG LAKE, NO wonder this hymn sprang to her mind. The mountains of the Many Glacier Valley of Glacier National Park are truly awesome—billion-year-old rock in bands of green and red, sculpted to jagged splendor by past glaciers. To Lorraine, the scenery was "Thy power throughout the Universe displayed."

The Many Glacier Road ends at Swiftcurrent Inn, where numerous hiking trails splinter off into the backcountry. It is fairly open country, with groves of aspen and evergreens giving way to miles of brushy slopes and alpine meadows. The valley is magnificent not only for its scenery, but also because it is home to some of North America's most magnificent creatures. In the summer, giant bull moose feed on water plants in the marshes and lakes, water pouring from their velvet antlers when they lift them above the surface. Burly bighorn rams peer down from scree fields, gazing down on all except the mountain goats and golden eagles. If you want to see a bear, the Many Glacier Valley is probably the best place in Montana to look for one. Not only is the valley well stocked with both black and grizzly bears, but because the animals feed in meadows and avalanche chutes, they are often visible from a safe distance.

Deane and Lorraine Lengkeek of Holland, Michigan, were not necessarily looking for a bear. On August 30, 1991, they simply wanted to hike to Iceberg Lake, enjoying a particularly choice segment of Glacier's 700 miles of hiking trails. Iceberg Lake is cupped in a sheer-wall amphitheater with cliffs rising 3,000 feet straight up from the water. A dying fragment of a glacier hangs over one edge of the lake. Ultra-fine glacial sediments suspended in the water give Iceberg Lake a striking turquoise color. The water is frigid and constantly teased by the mountain winds. Throughout much of the summer, miniature icebergs bob on the surface.

To reach Iceberg Lake, one must hike nearly five miles, climbing more than 1,000 vertical feet from the valley floor. But the trail is well groomed and gradual. Deane and Lorraine, both 62, were grandparents of fifteen kids but were in good physical condition and looked forward to the strenuous walk.

It was Friday. The summer rush of park visitors was tapering off as Labor Day Weekend approached. Deane and Lorraine had hiked for hours, marching steadily upward. To pass the time and to distract her mind from her body's toil, Lorraine sang one of her favorite hymns, *How Great Thou Art*.

About three in the afternoon, they had only about a half-hour more walking before they would reach the lake. At this point the trail quits climbing and descends slightly across a high slope. Deane wore a packsack with lunch and water. Around her neck Lorraine wore a full-size pair of seven-power binoculars. Occasionally she would stop and scan the mountains. She never saw the bears until it was too late. Even so, those binoculars came in very handy indeed.

●　●　●

DEANE WALKED in the lead. He noticed motion perhaps fifty feet downhill from the trail. His eyes focused on one bear—and then two others. It was a mother bear with two yearling cubs. Hiking in bear country is a bit like shooting dice. Thousands upon thousands of people hike to Iceberg Lake every summer. Most never see a bear, let alone have a dangerous encounter with one. But Deane had rolled snake eyes.

With a *woof,* the mother bear sent the cubs scurrying away. Then she chomped her teeth and charged. There was no time to even utter a shout before the bear tackled Deane. Lorraine dropped to the ground behind him and covered her head, playing dead.

Deane weighed 190 pounds, but the bear easily flipped him over and knocked off his backpack. She began biting his right shoulder, arm, and the side of his torso. He winced in pain with every bite. He knew the advised strategy in these circumstances was to play dead, but the instinct to fight back was overpowering.

"I thought I was going to die there on that hill," Deane later told a newspaper reporter. "I remembered my family and thought, this is not the way I want to die, being torn apart by a bear."

Lorraine, meanwhile, was on the ground listening to the sounds of the attacking bear and the cries of her husband.

"After hearing him cry for help and hearing the bear's teeth going into his flesh, I just couldn't lay there any more," Lorraine said. "I could hear Deane screaming and I knew he wasn't playing dead anymore. I looked out of the corner of my eye and could see the bear pulling and chomping on him. I thought:

You dirty bird. You're not going to get him without fighting me to the very end."

Lorraine stood up to her full five-foot, four inches. At 130 pounds, she was a bit like David standing down a shaggy Goliath. But instead of a sling and five smooth stones, she had a pair of binoculars.

Lorraine took the strap in one hand and swung the binoculars overhead, landing the heavy metal and glass squarely on the bear's head. "I was mad and I just whacked him four times, as fast as my arm could go around."

As Lorraine's arm swung around the fifth time, the bear looked up from Deane to Lorraine. The bear and the human—both fiercely defending their kin—locked eyes. The bear dropped Deane's arm, woofed once again, then turned tail and ran. Goliath had enough.

*   *   *

THE BEAR WAS GONE, but Deane was still in danger. The bear had raked his arms, chest, and shoulder. He was losing blood, fast. Lorraine looked up and down the trail and shouted for help, but no one was in sight. The nearest road was four miles away and the nearest medical clinic many miles beyond that.

Lorraine treated her husband's wounds as best she could. She shrugged out of her brassiere and fashioned a tourniquet to stop the bleeding from the worst of the lacerations.

After twenty minutes, Lorraine heard voices. More hikers were coming down the trail. A visitor from West Germany saw the trouble and took off running for help. He encountered other hikers who happened to be nurses and rescue volunteers; they rushed to help. Eventually, Park Ranger Jim White arrived on horseback. He had good news—the ALERT medical helicopter was en route from the Kalispell Regional Medical Center.

Minutes later, the red Bell helicopter crested the Continental Divide, touching down in a nearby meadow. As the chopper's rotors slowed, the rescue crew scrambled out in their blue flight suits with first aid packs and a stretcher. Together, rangers and the ALERT team loaded Deane into the helicopter and flew to the hospital. After surgery and some blood transfusions, Deane was out of danger.

The couple gave bedside interviews from Deane's hospital room. Their story burned across the Associated Press wire. "She saved my life," Deane told reporters. "She had the strength and the bravery to do it. We're just happy to be alive."

Instantly Lorraine became a Montana folk hero—the grandmother who fought off a bear attack with little more than her bare hands. An advertising firm hired Lorraine in a series of magazine commercials for Timex watches. Her moxie seemed to reflect the company's slogan, "Takes a licking and keeps on ticking."

* * *

TWO UNANSWERED QUESTIONS followed the incident. One, was the attacking bear a grizzly or a black bear? Two, is it wise for an unarmed person to fight back when attacked by a defensive mother bear?

We will never know the certain answer to the first question. Deane and Lorraine did not have enough experience with bears to positively determine which species attacked, and there was insufficient evidence at the scene to tell for certain.

Big black bears in Montana can grow to 300 pounds, which is every bit as big as an average female Rocky Mountain grizzly. In Montana, grizzly bears have a much more fierce reputation than do black bears. In fact, black bears are almost regarded as comic clowns. That doesn't give black bears the respect that they deserve. Across North America, experts say black bears kill about five people a year. Grizzlies, on the other hand, kill only one or two people an average year. Part of the reason behind those statistics is the fact that black bears are far more common than grizzlies. Black bears also exist in places like New Jersey and California, which have far more people than the Montana wilderness.

Most black bears flee like a shot at the first sight or scent of people. But black bears can be bold and even dangerous, particularly when they lose their natural fear of humans and become addicted to human food. In 2001, a black bear broke into a rural home in rural New Mexico and killed an elderly woman who lived there. Yet in Glacier, no black bears have ever killed anyone. If a black bear has ever killed anyone in Montana, it's been lost to history.

In June 2000, a black bear at Glacier's Two Medicine Lake attacked an airman visiting from Malmstrom Air Force Base, biting the airman on the shoulder. Investigating rangers found that attack was unprovoked but knew the bear had earlier lost its fear of humans. Before that attack, the most recent confirmed black bear attack in Glacier took place in 1978 when a camper was bitten by a food-spoiled bear at Trout Lake.

At the time of the Lengkeek attack, Glacier National Park biologist Gary Gregory figured Lorraine bashed a black bear, not a grizzly. "It would be a rarity to hit a grizzly female in the nose with a pair of binoculars and not pay for it," Gregory said in a newspaper article that week. "I've not heard of that happening before. Usually, a grizzly female protecting cubs will keep fighting as long as there is still something fighting her. The case sounds like it was a black bear."

Regardless of the species, the Lengkeeks experienced a classic surprise encounter. Even though they were making noise by singing, they evidently caught the mother bear unaware and at close quarters. The mother bear took them for a threat to her cubs and charged.

Here's what experts say to do in a surprise encounter: First, stand your ground. Fight your instinct to run. If the bear charges at all, the animal is probably bluffing and will abort the charge, stopping short or swerving away. If you carry pepper spray, hose down the bear with the stuff, aiming for its nose and mouth.

If the charge becomes an attack, drop facedown to the ground. Curl your arms over your head and lay flat on the ground to protect your chest, keeping your backpack on to protect your back. Then, grit your teeth and take the punishment as best as you can. Most often, the bear will stop its attack as soon as it senses its foe is not resisting. A defensive bear's goal isn't to kill but to protect. Once the bear believes its job is done, it will most likely leave the scene. Experts like Glacier Chief Ranger Steve Frye say fighting back during a surprise encounter often makes maulings worse.

This advice is vastly different from what to do with a food-conditioned bear, be it a black bear or a grizzly. These bears are particularly dangerous because they may see people as prey. If a bear comes into camp or approaches a cabin, try to scare it off. Don't take any unnecessary risks, but throw rocks or pound pots and pans to haze the animal. If the animal attacks—for example, ripping through a tent to get at campers sleeping inside—fight back with whatever weapon is at hand.

Of course, the best bet is to avoid bear trouble in the first place. The basic rules for avoiding bears are: Hike in groups, hike in the middle of the day, stay alert for bear sign, and make plenty of noise. These actions decrease your odds of a bear encounter, but they can't eliminate the chance. You'll notice that Deane Lengkeek was not alone, was hiking in mid-afternoon, and was making noise by singing. Sometimes, hikers like Deane and Lorraine follow all the rules but meet trouble anyway. Sometimes, you roll snake eyes.

Boundless Enthusiasm for Bears

WHEN IT COMES TO GRIZZLY BEARS, TIM RUBBERT AND JIM COLE cannot get enough. Not tonight. Not ever.

It is May and grubby snow is retreating from the mountains. Glacier National Park crews have plowed this section of Going-to-the-Sun Road, but it remains closed to cars. The evening breeze alternates warm off the asphalt then cool off the snowfields. In the south-facing avalanche chutes, snow is beginning to be replaced by the vivid green of spring bear food. On the distant slope roams a lanky grizzly, thin from hibernation. A few hundred yards below it, a female grizzly scratches an ear with a rear paw. Her cub is balled up asleep next to her.

"Those slopes look just perfect," says Rubbert, lifting his head from behind his spotting scope. "There have got to be more bears up there."

Cole and Rubbert met by chance. They both grew up in the Midwest, watching *Wild Kingdom* and *National Geographic* specials on television. They both had youthful dreams of being wildlife biologists, later scrubbed for more practical careers. They both abandoned lucrative city jobs to live near the Montana wilderness. When the two of them see bears, energy bounces between them like electrons between supercharged particles.

Both men are athletic and bearded. Rubbert lives near White-fish within a short drive to Glacier National Park. Cole lives in Bozeman within striking distance of Yellowstone National Park. Rubbert teaches handicapped folks to downhill ski during the winter. He is taller and more reserved. Cole, a former tennis pro and Realtor, is more compact and more animated, telling his bear stories with both hands. This evening, they pedaled on their mountain bicycles to this bear-watching spot on Going-to-the-Sun Road. It's too early for the tourist crowds, but a few park visitors also bicycle past. The others chat among themselves and gawk at the mountains, but Cole and Rubbert remain focused.

"Our lives revolve around watching bears," said Cole. "It is by far our greatest interest, besides our families and friends."

To gauge their obsession, consider that in a typical year Rubbert and Cole see between 100 and 300 grizzly bears in and around Glacier and Yellowstone national parks. They've found grizzly tracks every month of the year and have seen bears from March through November.

Granted, they no doubt count some bears more than once. But their tallies represent a lot of bears by any measure, especially when you consider there are fewer than 1,000 grizzlies in the lower forty-eight states. They photograph bears if they're close enough. Mostly, though, they watch through binoculars and spotting scopes.

Cole clearly remembers seeing his first grizzly bear—a female with cubs—on a Glacier visit more than twenty years before. "Grizzly bears have an undeniable mystique," Cole said. "It's a whole different world when you are out among grizzlies. You have to be on your game. Their presence heightens your awareness."

"I think it's simple," Rubbert said. "Grizzly bears are the epitome of pure wilderness. Their beauty, their grace, and their power is unmatched by any animal I've ever seen in the wild."

Rubbert and Cole's days together are often dawn-to-dusk bear-a-thons. It's not unusual for them to hike twenty miles a day to look for bruins.

"Our careers watching bears both really turned a corner when we met each other," Cole said. "I had never met anyone who shared my enthusiasm in the same way. My learning curve started to get really sharp when I started spending field time with Tim."

They work as a team. When one spots a distant bear with binoculars, he keeps track of it while the other sets up a tripod and spotting scope. They take turns watching the bear and scanning for more. It's not unusual for them to find several bears a day. Of course, it's not usual not to see any, either. "We definitely pay our dues," Rubbert said.

They are still at it—even after a scare that might have frightened other folk out of grizzly country for good.

*   *   *

SOME OF THEIR MOST SUCCESSFUL BEAR-WATCHING occurs in the autumn. The hordes of summer tourists have left bear country and the world is ablaze in fall colors. The sky tends to be clear, the atmosphere sharp, and the air filled with a bracing coolness. The bears are in peak condition and tend to spend much more time feeding during daylight hours as they sense winter coming. During this period of seasonal gorging that biologists call "hyperphagia," a bear may consume 20,000 calories in a single autumn day.

On September 29, 1993, Cole and Rubbert planned to hike to Fifty Mountain, deep in Glacier's backcountry. Fifty Mountain's west flank is a long, gently sloping open hillside. It's the nearest thing to tundra in the Montana Rockies. In the summer, little yellow flowers called glacier lilies bloom in the meadows. These plants store energy in special roots called corms. Grizzly bears love digging for corms with their long, badger-like claws, then nipping off the tasty morsels. Fifty Mountain's slopes look like teams of deranged gardeners with Roto-tillers have attacked them.

Cole and Rubbert knew Fifty Mountain would be a good place to see bears, but they had to cover a lot of ground to get there. Most people make Fifty Mountain a two- or three-day trip. It's a challenging, twelve-mile hike from the nearest road. Cole and Rubbert planned to crank-out the full twenty-four miles roundtrip in a single day, starting at Packer's Roost on the Going-to-the-Sun Road and going to Fifty Mountain via the Flattop Mountain Trail. Just after the fall equinox, they had about twelve hours of daylight. To make it there and back before dark, they would have to start early and keep moving nearly all day, stopping only to snack and glass for bears.

* * *

GLACIER NATIONAL PARK IS HOME to perhaps 200 to 300 grizzly bears. Every year, between 1.5 and 2 million people visit the park, the largest numbers in July and August. Every year, one or two of those visitors gets mauled. That's on average. Some summers, no one is hurt by a bear. Other summers as many as four hikers may, as the rangers put it, "get nailed." It's the unlucky one-in-a-million hiker who gets mauled by a grizzly.

Statistically, waterfalls, cars, cold lakes, and avalanches have each maimed and killed more Glacier visitors than bears ever have or ever will. But bear attacks are what visitors think about when they start down a trail. Big red signs at every park entrance and trailhead warn visitors they are entering grizzly country. And the grizzly leaves its own signs—tracks in snow banks and claw marks on pine trees. Walk very far on Glacier's trails and you'll soon step over a big, berry-filled pile of grizzly scat. The grizzly's presence is palpable.

Most attacks in Glacier are what rangers call "surprise encounters." A hiker walks down a trail through thick brush or along a burbling creek. He comes around a corner and bumps into a bear at close range. The bear is a female with cubs, or perhaps a lone bear standing over a winter-killed mountain goat. Most often, the bear flees. Other times, the bear bluff-charges. Sometimes the bear attacks.

A few times, the attacks are fatal. But most of the time, the surprised bear doesn't kill anyone. This is a remarkable fact given that a bear could snap a human's neck with little more effort than it takes a person to snap a pencil. But time and again, if the victim doesn't fight back, the bear will bite, scratch, and even sit on a person, but then leave. It seems that once the bear has achieved its goal of demobilizing the perceived threat, the animal will back off. This knowledge, of course, does little to mitigate the pure terror one must feel when a quarter-ton of fury bursts toward you at racehorse speed.

•   •   •

COLE AND RUBBERT WERE IN GOOD SHAPE after a summer in the mountains, and they reached Fifty Mountain in the middle of that glorious, Indian summer day. They continued past the little campground to a high pass where they could see for miles. They glassed the high slopes and made photographs of the places where bears had fed. But for all their miles and eye-strain, they had not seen a single bear. The afternoon had topped seventy degrees, and they had hiked in shorts and T-shirts. The bears, however, were clad in a layer of fat and thick autumn coats. They were spending the afternoon hidden in the shade.

It was such a beautiful day the men were only a bit disappointed they hadn't seen a bear. After lunch, Rubbert and Cole shouldered their packs and left Fifty Mountain to hike the twelve miles back to the car. Rubbert led the hike from the road, so Cole took the lead going back. Even though they didn't plan to spend the night, they carried backpacks that weighed forty pounds apiece. Besides extra clothing, food, water, and survival gear, they carried cameras, telephoto lenses, and other gear. The trail back to their car climbed over Kootenai Pass, then crossed over Flattop Mountain and dropped toward Flattop Creek. They had not seen much bear sign, but they stopped occasionally to glass the mountain slopes. It looked like it would be one of those bearless days paying their dues.

On the broad bench that is the summit of Flattop Mountain, the trail crossed a glade broken up with scattered subalpine firs. The two friends argued good-naturedly about professional football. (Rubbert is a Minnesota Vikings fan, while Cole is devoted to the Chicago Bears.) Cole walked perhaps forty feet ahead of Rubbert.

"All of a sudden I heard a huffing," Cole said. "I looked up and saw the beautiful face of a light-colored, subadult grizzly bear, barreling right towards me at point blank range. There was no time to think. There was no time for fear. There was no time to wonder where Tim was, or what I was going to do. I started to turn away, but the bear was on me in an instant."

Rubbert heard the noise, too. He called it more of a hiss than a huff. It reminded him of a locomotive letting off steam. "As soon as I heard it, before I even lifted my eyes, I thought, 'Oh boy, here we go.' It was a sound full of intensity and desperation."

From there, Cole's memory of the attack begins to fog. The bear's roundhouse blows reminded Rubbert of a boxer. Cole succeeded in dodging one or two swipes before falling to the ground.

"I hollered at Jim to get down, but he had no choice. He was already on his way down," Rubbert said. In an instant, the bear planted Cole firmly on the ground, pinning him with one paw on his back. The bear took the back of Cole's head into its mouth and ripped his scalp open. Instinctively Cole covered his head with his hands. The bear bit into his left hand.

"I always wondered how fast I could draw my can of pepper spray," Rubbert said. "It was just instantaneous. I flicked off the safety tab and took a couple steps back."

Rubbert was about forty feet from the bear. He figured it was a young bear, perhaps four years old, and weighed perhaps 250 pounds. The bear had its back to Rubbert and was biting Cole's hip. Rubbert figured the bear had no clue Rubbert was there but would turn on him as soon as it made the discovery.

"I was thinking clearly, but I had no choices. I just wanted to get the bear's attention." Rubbert fired a quick burst of the red mist toward the bear. He succeeded in distracting the animal, like a rodeo clown distracts a Brahma bull.

As the bruin charged Rubbert, he let loose with the full force of his pepper spray. The bear slammed face-first into the red-hot capsicum mist about five feet shy of Rubbert. Rubbert kept spraying until the can began to dribble dry. The bear aborted the attack and fled downslope.

Rubbert asked if Cole was okay. Cole stood up, blood sheeting from his lacerated scalp. At least he could stand. The two men moved away from the attack site. Cole tore his first aid kit out of his pack and dumped the contents on the ground. Adrenaline was pumping through Cole's veins. Now they reviewed their predicament, replaying the mental tapes and trying to figure out what to do next. The two men wondered if the bear would return. Rubbert feared it might, but Cole figured the bear was gone.

At that point it was three-fifteen in the afternoon. The two men were more than ten miles from the road. This time of year, it was very unlikely anyone else would be on the trail for days, or even the rest of the year.

"Jim's head was bleeding profusely," Rubbert recalled. "He had an inch-wide gash that started at his forehead and continued over the top of his head. I was thinking, this could be bad. I didn't want to leave him out there."

Cole gritted his teeth as Rubbert poured hydrogen peroxide into the gash. They used gauze and tape to wrap Cole's hand and swaddled his head in gauze, an ace bandage, and a T-shirt. Cole looked like he was wearing a bloody turban. Rubbert had seen the bear take a mighty bite at Cole's hip. Cole was wearing a camera with a telephoto lens on a padded hip holster. The bear's teeth had broken the camera, but the camera had absorbed the bite and protected Cole from crippling injuries.

Cole was in sorry shape to be walking anywhere, let alone ten rugged miles to the truck. Waiting out a long, dark night, bleeding and wounded in bear country, wasn't much of an option. Rubbert took the heaviest items out of Cole's pack: His camera, binoculars, and scope. "We took some pictures to document the site, then got the hell out of there," Rubbert said. "By then it was about three-thirty in the afternoon."

Cole marched down the trail ahead of Rubbert. Fueled by adrenaline, Cole left Rubbert behind with the heavy load. Every now and then, Cole felt moisture seeping down the back of his neck. He felt with his hand to brush away the sweat, but when he withdrew his hand it dripped with blood.

The men covered roughly four miles in a couple of hours. Downhill sections were easy enough, but uphill pitches were killers. At the top of one hill, Rubbert found Cole sitting on the side of the trail, hanging his bloodied head. Cole was growing exhausted. Rubbert took the rest of Cole's load and tied it to his own pack with rope. Rubbert was now carrying around eighty pounds. He helped Cole to his feet and they started again toward safety.

Again Cole went ahead as Rubbert plodded under his load.

After two more miles, Rubbert again caught up with Cole. This time Cole was lying in the middle of the trail. He couldn't get up. He appeared to be utterly spent. The adrenaline, wounds, shock, loss of blood, and the miles of hard hiking had taken their toll. Cole sat on the forest floor, unable to go further. They were in deep woods now, a jungle of brush. There was no place a rescue helicopter could land. Darkness was closing in.

"This is when I really started to worry," Rubbert said. "I really didn't know what was going on. It was really thick in there and I didn't want to leave him."

It occurred to them that they had not eaten anything since lunch more than six hours earlier. In Rubbert's pack they found energy bars and Gatorade. After the calories kicked in, Cole found he could regain his feet and resume the retreat.

The route from there was mostly downhill. Just as it was getting too dark to see, the men broke out of the timber and found Tim's vehicle. They got in and Tim drove as fast as he could to West Glacier, where he stopped at a pay phone to call the Kalispell hospital. A vacationing doctor happened to be using a pay phone nearby and overheard the conversation. He quickly checked Cole's vital signs and sent him on his way. Rubbert climbed back behind the wheel and the two sped toward town.

State highway police had been alerted the men were coming and let Rubbert speed down U.S. Highway 2. When his van pulled up to the emergency room at Kalispell Regional Medical Center, a local television cameraman was waiting.

"I did not want to be photographed in that condition," Cole said. "It was just additional sensationalism that doesn't help anybody."

The cameraman respected Cole's privacy. Inside, the doctors X-rayed Cole's wrist and treated the broken bones. They stapled shut the gashes in his scalp. The television reporter hung around, so Rubbert gave an interview. Cole gave more interviews once his head was bandaged and cleaned up. The pain would not slam into him until more than twenty-four hours after the attack. Later he got a get-well note from a friend in Uruguay who had read of Cole's attack in *USA Today*.

* * *

LOOKING BACK, Cole figures the attack was a classic surprise encounter. The bear probably made a day bed in the patch of fir next to the trail. That time of year, few people were using the trail and the bear probably thought he had the mountain to himself. The men happened into the bear's bedroom, startling it out of a sleep.

Certainly Cole and Rubbert are not typical Glacier tourists. They actively seek out bears and are quite skilled at finding them. Cole figures he has walked 12,000 miles in grizzly habitat—often habitat fairly saturated with bears. He does not walk in fear of bears. He stays alert to bear sign as a matter of habit. When passing through brushy woods or dense forest full of bear sign or bear food, he makes noise to avoid surprising a bear. But he doesn't shout all the time, nor does he bother with bear bells.

The attack didn't dampen the men's enthusiasm for bears and bear country. But it did make them more conscious of the ace that Rubbert held in his hand that day: bear pepper spray.

Starting in the early 1990s, marketers began selling pepper spray designed expressly for repelling grizzlies. One of the first products was Counter Assault developed by Montana entrepreneur Bill Pounds along with field and laboratory testing by biologists Chuck Jonkel and Carrie Hunt. In the 1970s, Pounds was a Vietnam War vet cruising America on his motorcycle. He rode over Glacier National Park's Going-to-the-Sun Road and camped alongside Hungry Horse Reservoir. He heard noises outside his tent the entire night and didn't sleep a minute, believing hungry bears lurked in the dark.

Pounds fell in love with grizzly country, but his combat experience left him with a high need for a sense of security. He didn't want to be burdened with a loaded 12-gauge shotgun. He figured there had to be a better way of stopping a bear's charge than blowing holes in the bear. He set about developing one.

While traveling in Mexico, Pounds learned about capsicum pepper—a natural pepper that is more than 400 times more potent than the hottest jalapeño. He figured out a way to distill capsicum and convert it into a potent spray. Today, Counter Assault shares the shelf with several competing pepper sprays.

Pepper spray is widely gaining favor in bear country. It's lighter and less expensive than a sidearm and is easy enough for nearly any adult to use. Plus, guns are illegal in national parks. What's more, pepper spray doesn't kill the offending bear but rather leaves it smarter to avoid humans another day. There are literally scores of examples where bear spray has evidently stopped attacks, and—unlike firearms—no cases in which pepper spray made an attack worse.

Pounds believes that pepper spray overpowers bears with more than pain alone. Charged up on adrenaline and rage, a bear's pain threshold may be virtually impossible to exceed. Instead, Pounds believes the vaporized pepper mist makes it difficult for the bear to breathe. The effect is something like holding someone's head underwater—it immediately grabs the bear's attention, breaking off the very *idea* of the attack in the bear's head.

Both Rubbert and Cole swear by the stuff. Rubbert emphasizes that pepper spray is not a replacement for common sense in bear country, or an excuse to do risky or stupid things around bears.

Rubbert and Cole were eager to get back in bear country when Cole healed. "The attack really didn't change our activities all that much," Rubbert said. "We love it too much to stop. We knew the risks going in. I still don't believe we take unnecessary risks."

Rubbert has made one change since the attack: Now he packs *two* cans of pepper spray. "Anybody who spends time in grizzly country should carry it," Cole concurs. "It's cheap insurance. But at the same time, nothing is 100 percent effective, all the time."

Of Dogs and Bears

STAN ANDERSON TAKES A DAILY WALK IN THE WOODS FOR HIS HEALTH. He does so even though one of his walks turned out very unhealthy indeed.

Stan credits his oversized Labrador retriever with saving his life from an angry mother black bear. Stan was lucky. In other circumstances, mixing dogs, bears, and people can trigger disaster. When it comes to bears, a dog can be a savior, or a dog can trigger a hiker's worst nightmare.

Stan is a retired high school teacher from the sawmill town of Eureka, in far northwest Montana. Stan lives about ten miles south of town in a rural, forested area known as Pinkham Creek. It is prime wildlife country. Stan has seen moose in his front yard. Once a black bear climbed on his porch to raid a cache of dog food. (Stan has since learned to lock dog food inside, where bears won't find it.)

Stan shares his home with Ole, a 140-pound chocolate Lab. Yes, that's right: *one hundred forty pounds*. The dog is built on a large frame and has a glandular problem as well. Ole is a giant dog with a giant heart. He wouldn't make much of a bird dog, as he is sometimes frightened silly by the sound of a grouse taking flight.

"He is a very gentle, compassionate, and kind dog," Stan said. "Sometimes, he chases moths, but then it's just the shadow of the moths."

Stan is very fond of Ole. And vice versa. Every day Stan

loads Ole in the 1980 Chevy Chevette that Stan has dubbed the Ole-mobile. The dog's tail spins like a carnival ride in anticipation. They drive to a promising spot in the forest and walk a couple of miles, perhaps exploring the ruins of some old logging camp or mining town along the way.

One June day in 1999, the routine started out as expected. The day was sunny and long, a delightful foretaste of summer. It was the kind of day when black bears edge out of the forest shadows to feed on the fresh grass and clover that sprouts alongside logging roads.

Ole took his usual place at heel and the two walked down the forest road. It was pleasant, easy walking, each twist and turn in the road luring them on to discover what might be around the bend. After they had walked about a mile, Stan saw a small black animal dash across the road. Even though the image was gone in a split second, Stan identified it as a bear cub.

"I said, 'Ole, let's get out of here. That cub's momma can't be too far away.'"

So they did just that. They turned right around and walked away. They walked at a normal pace—there seemed no reason to hurry. Ole remained at Stan's side the entire time.

A short ways down the road, Stan heard a scuffling sound behind him. He turned on his heel—just in time to see the mother black bear barreling down the road straight for him.

"If I had been carrying a pistol or a can of pepper spray, it wouldn't have done me a lick of good," Stan said. "A 45-millimeter Howitzer would have done me no good. She was just too fast."

The bear reached out with a forepaw and slapped Stan across his forehead. The claws caught flesh at the edge of his right eye and Stan was immediately half-blinded by his own blood. "I didn't want to fight back too much initially," Stan said. "I thought that might make it worse. I did yell at her real good."

Ole had his own designs. The dog ducked low, staying out of the bear's line of sight. Once behind the bear, Ole chomped his teeth into the bear's hide. As Stan recalled: "Ole got behind her and bit her in the...umm...bit her in the lower posterior region."

Stan was still on his feet. After a brief tussle between the bear and the dog, the bear fled back toward its cub. Stan and Ole turned around and started walking toward the car, still a mile away. This time, there was more urgency in their step.

"I was bleeding like a stuck hog," Stan said. "I couldn't see out of my right eye for all the blood. I thought she got my eye."

So with one hand cupped over his face, Stan kept moving toward his car. Ole remained at his side. Then Stan again heard the sound of the bear running toward them. He turned around—and here came a second charge.

"She was just a disagreeable-looking beast," Stan said. "When I was a kid, I used to watch werewolf movies. That's what she reminded me of."

"This time she knocked me to my knees. She got my shoulder in her teeth and then began happily chomping on my elbow. I knew darned well she would go for my throat next."

Once again, Ole skirted round the bear's backside and bit her hard in the "lower posterior region." Again, the bear stopped her attack and ran back toward her cub. This time Stan's wounds were more serious.

"My injuries didn't seem to hurt, yet," Stan said. "I wanted to get back to my car as quickly as I could."

The adrenaline charging through Stan's veins temporarily shut down the pain receptors in his nerves. He was able to keep moving. The bear never came back.

Stan was relieved when he started seeing again out of his right eye—he hadn't lost it after all. Finally, the man and dog made it back to the Chevette. Stan got behind the wheel and, his hands shaking from shock and sticky with his own blood, turned the ignition. He put the car in gear and drove the twenty minutes or so back home, passing no other cars. Before he could reach help, Stan started feeling himself growing woozy from blood loss. He was blacking out. He felt his head start to loll about on his neck but was powerless to control it.

Suddenly he woke to something wet and cold against his face. Once again, Ole came to the rescue. This time the dog licked his owner's face until Stan snapped alert. Stan pulled into a neighbor's driveway and honked the horn. His neighbor took the wheel and rushed Stan to the clinic in Eureka. Stan went from there to larger hospitals for two days of surgery and antibiotics. Although Stan still bears scars from the attack, he is nearly 100 percent recovered, both emotionally and physically. Ole and Stan still enjoy their regular walks through the woods.

* * *

DOGS AND BEARS SHARE AN ANCIENT ANIMOSITY. All of our common breeds of dogs are descended from domesticated wolves. Wolves are known to attack and kill both black and grizzly bears. In the 1990s, a pilot and a wildlife biologist flying over Glacier National Park watched a pack of eighteen wolves surround and harry a mother grizzly, trying to isolate and kill her cub. The animals disappeared into the timber so no one knows how that episode concluded. Similar events happened countless times over millions of years. No wonder bears seem to carry a grudge.

Some dogs carry the instinct to attack bears. If the bear stands its ground or chases after the dog, the dog may seek backup from the rest of its "pack." When this happens, they come running back to their owners, often with a bear fast on their tails. The bears are hopped up on their own defensive instincts. When they follow the dog into people, they may lash out. Canadian bear expert Stephen Herrero put it this way: "The right dog can be a valuable extension of your senses in bear country. …But only a well-trained dog, experienced around bears, is an advantage to its owner. An untrained dog can trigger an attack."

That's part of the reason why dogs are not allowed on trails in national parks. There are no rules banning dogs from Montana's national forests. However, experts agree that if one elects to take a dog into wildlife country, the pet should be under firm control, preferably on a leash. This not only prevents a run-in with a bear but also prevents the dog from chasing deer, getting nailed by a porcupine, or getting sprayed by a skunk.

●　●　●

A MORE TYPICAL BEAR-DOG CLASH came in late July 1998 between Whitefish resident Bob Brown, his male, black-and-white Karelian bear dog, Mishka, and a young grizzly. The Karelian bear dog is a Finnish/ Russian breed developed for hunting brown bears, moose, and other large mammals. In the United States, specially trained Karelian bear dogs are used to haze black and grizzly bears out of campgrounds in places like Yosemite and Glacier national parks. In fact, Brown selected the breed because he figured Mishka might protect his daughters from mountain lions and bears near their home. Brown acknowledges that Mishka had all the instincts of a bear-hunter but none of the formalized training.

Brown planned to fly-fish for cutthroat trout at Swift Creek north of Whitefish Lake. At the moment, they weren't exactly fishing. Rather, they were fighting their way through thick downed logs and heavy brush to reach the creek where Brown could try a few casts and get a drink of water. Brown was getting tired and his thoughts were on reaching water. Brown had fished that stream for years and had never seen a grizzly in the area. Mishka was running nearby, most of the time out of sight in the thick brush. Brush-beaten and weary, Brown sat on the ground to catch his breath and orient himself. He sat there, slapping mosquitoes.

"It was hot, it was buggy, and I was feeling sorry for myself," Brown said. Once he sat still, though, Brown could hear the burbling creek. He knew he was close to his destination.

"Then I heard a sound that I had never heard before," Brown said. "It was a sharp, cracking, hacking sound. It was a big, shocking sound. I was thinking, what is that? A moose?"

Brown heard crashing in the bushes about thirty yards away. He looked up to see Mishka running toward him. Hard on the dog's tail was a full-grown grizzly.

"It was a big, lanky, spidery, taffy-colored grizzly bear, and it was right on top of that dog," Brown said. The dog dodged the bear's swiping paws and headed straight for Brown. The forest was so thick that Brown had barely been able to force his way through it, but the bear appeared to glide effortlessly through the tangled brush.

"The dog came right back to daddy and when he did the bear followed the dog straight toward me," Brown said. "I saw the bear's eyes see me. Then he came for me, instead of the dog."

Without thinking twice, Brown shot up the nearest tree, a spindly lodgepole pine about five inches in diameter. "I didn't stop to think, 'I wonder if I am capable of climbing this tree?' I was up that tree in about two seconds."

"The bear got to the base of the tree just when I was out of his reach," Brown said. "He reached way up with his paws, but he didn't roar or snarl or do anything menacing. He stood up on his hind legs and reached up with its claws. His claws were about one foot below the bottoms of my boots. I looked right down into the face of that bear."

Time is hard to judge under such circumstances, but Brown estimates the bear was directly under the tree for about a minute and within sight for perhaps ten minutes. The bear circled the tree curiously. The dog, meanwhile, remained nearby but didn't bark or otherwise aggravate the bear.

"I was afraid I would lose my grip on the tree because I was getting tired," Brown said. "Remember, I was tired before this whole thing started."

Eventually the bear wandered off and Brown slid to the ground. His legs were skinned by the bark, but he was otherwise okay. Mishka sulked back, his tail drooping.

"I picked up my rod and walking stick and circled away from the bear as quickly and as quietly as I could. I felt totally vulnerable. I was totally in the bear's domain. I was about as defenseless against that bear as a rabbit would be against me."

He and Mishka reached the creek where Brown finally got his drink of water. He even made a few casts for trout but thought better of it and decided to leave in case the bear was still nearby.

At the time of the attack, Brown had served in the Montana Senate for more than twenty years. A skilled politician, Brown knows a good story when he lives through one. The next day he was showing his skinned knees and hands to a broadcaster and newspaper reporter in Kalispell. In 2000, Brown was elected Montana's Secretary of State. An abridged version of his bear story is on the office's official website, under "About Bob Brown."

For the bear's part, the animal probably lingered in the creek bottom because it was a cool, secluded spot to lay low through the heat of the afternoon. It was probably in a day bed, perhaps near a food supply, when the dog routed it out. Once Brown was up the tree, the bear certainly could have pushed over a five-inch lodgepole pine, but the bear didn't want any more trouble.

Brown still fishes Swift Creek but never alone. Both he and his fishing partner carry bear pepper spray and a sidearm. Brown pays more attention to bear sign in the woods. Moreover, he leaves Mishka at home.

"You know, if I took that dog out and ran into another bear and I got mauled, no one would feel the least bit sorry for me. Nor should they."

"I suppose the lesson you learn is to be careful," Brown said. "The forces of nature are powerful and there's always a possibility that you'll see a creature such as a grizzly bear in this country."

• • •

FEW PEOPLE HAVE MORE EXPERIENCE WITH DOGS AND BEARS THAN Carrie Hunt of the Wind River Bear Institute. Hunt is a pioneer in the emerging practice of "bear shepherding." Essentially, Hunt and biologists trained in human-bear conflict use a highly trained pack of Karelian bear dogs to teach bears to recognize and avoid human boundaries, such as campgrounds and ranches. They also teach people how to properly store potential attractants and to behave in bear country. The barking dogs are backed up with rubber bullets, pepper spray, and other unpleasantries. Bears are naturally territorial and can learn to stay away from places. If people remove garbage and store food properly, bears stay out of trouble. This saves bears' lives.

Based in Utah, Hunt travels throughout North America. She has worked in national parks, including Glacier and Yellowstone, with both grizzly and black bears. Her team "pushes or teaches" bears in 200 to 300 cases a year, most often grizzlies and often at quite close range. Never has a bear injured a dog or a handler, nor have the people had to injure or kill a bear to protect themselves.

Karelians are handsome dogs with pointed ears, a tight-curled tail, and distinctive black-and-white patterns. Hunt's work has helped make the breed famous in the United States, but Hunt says most people should forget the idea that Karelian bear dogs will make good household pets. Karelian bear dogs are genetically hard-wired to be courageous, far-ranging hounds. They are also notorious barkers and often run away from homes. They demand a lot of attention and exercise.

"The breed is intelligent, intense, and full of boundless energy," she said. "They are not a dog for the casual pet owner. A Karelian bear dog is not happy when confined. They need to work.

"And don't expect to go down the street on your bicycle or up the trail with a Karelian bear dog trotting beside you. The dog is going to be gone. They are a hunting dog bred for years to leave you."

When Hunt works bears, the dogs are never allowed to chase the bears. Both dogs and handlers wear harnesses and are tied together at all times.

"The reason we are able to work with bears safely is because we give the bears a lesson they understand. We make leaving the easiest option," Hunt said. "The dogs are our safety net in delivering the lesson. But they are in our control at all times. It requires a lot of discipline."

But what of the casual camper, hiker, or dog owner? Should they leave their dog behind?

Hunt says a well-trained, well-controlled dog of almost any breed can be a benefit in bear country. Hunt emphasizes that dogs should be under absolute control. A free-ranging dog is asking for trouble with bears and other wildlife. However, Hunt believes that a dog on a leash, or that stays close to hikers and comes when called, may help deter a bear or prevent a sudden encounter by alerting its owner to a bear's presence.

Moreover, she says dogs deter curious bears from entering camp. Bears don't like to attract attention, and a growling or barking dog can keep bears away from ranch headquarters, camps, and rural homes. But again, Hunt emphasizes the dog must remain at camp to be useful. A dog that tends to roam should be tied up.

Camp-raiding bears—either black or grizzly—can become so hooked on human food they will tolerate a ruckus that would send a normal bear running for the nearest horizon. A severely "food-conditioned" bear may even ignore a barking dog, especially if the dog's bark is worse than its bite.

"Bears are very adept at reading a dog's body language," Hunt says. "They know if a dog is tied up or not. They know when a dog means business and when it's bluffing."

In short, there's no reason why a responsible dog owner shouldn't enjoy the company of a dog, outside of national parks. However, the dog owner has to keep the dog in firm control. Otherwise Fido may come running back to its master with a hot bear on its heels.

D.J., Queen of the Yaak

🐻

IN THE 1980S GRIZZLY BEARS IN MONTANA'S YAAK RIVER VALLEY existed mostly as rumor, and grizzly sightings were almost like encounters with Bigfoot. A fisherman reported a brown blur dashing across a logging road; a berry-picker saw a silver-tipped form streaking through a clearcut; a logger found a suspicious track in fast-melting snow. Firm evidence was hard to find.

In 1986 a graduate student named Tim Thier launched a radio-telemetry study of black bears, not grizzlies, in the remote and densely forested northwest corner of Montana. He figured there was only an off chance that he might see, let alone capture, a grizzly bear.

Early in his first trapping season Thier and a trapping partner cruised forest roads for likely places to set snares. On one of those roads, Thier spotted the fuzzy rear end of a bear, its head down in a lush patch of clover. He hit the brakes and two perplexed cubs glanced back at him. Then the mother bear glanced up and saw the truck. She gave a snort and bounded for cover. It was only then Thier identified the bears as grizzlies. His study quickly expanded from black bears to include their larger cousins.

Thier returned the next day and set a snare. Two days later he nabbed the female grizzly, her two young cubs hiding somewhere nearby. Thier crept in and thumped the mother bear with a tranquilizer dart. When she conked out, Thier outfitted her with a radio collar. That's how Thier met Donna Jean and thus began an adventure that would span thirteen years.

Donna Jean was one of five grizzlies Thier captured in his research. "When I started, people thought I was lucky if I would catch one grizzly," he recalled. "Two would be a miracle. Five was considered impossible. It was pretty good for a grad student just winging it, working on the cheap, buying Buckhorn beer to save money,"

Donna Jean's official number was 106, but no one called her that. The unspoken tradition of bear research is the person who first captures a bear gets to give it a nickname. So radio-collared bears are saddled with the names of dogs, girlfriends, and ex-wives' lawyers. A twin pair of chummy grizzly bear brothers were nicknamed Jake and Elwood, after the characters in the movie *The Blues Brothers*. Donna Jean was named after one of Thier's old flames.

Call the bear D.J., for short. Everyone up the Yaak did. Locals from the Golden Nugget bar at Sylvanite to the Dirty Shame Saloon at Yaak talked about her. Her snapshot is still thumbtacked to the wall at the Yaak Mercantile, the social epicenter of the Yaak Valley.

There are no real towns in the Yaak, just buildings clustered around the Golden Nugget, the Dirty Shame, and the Merc. The Merc and the Dirty Shame are thirty miles from Libby, the nearest official city. Yaak residents live in scattered and remote homes ranging from clapboard hovels owned by hermits to custom-built log mansions. D.J. fit well among the people of the Yaak, both the Yaak bears and people being a bit reclusive.

•   •   •

The Yaak is a wild, remote region and D.J. lived in the most wild and remote portions of the Yaak. Places like Burnt Creek, Seventeenmile Creek, Roderick Mountain, Clark Peak, and most fittingly, Grizzly Peak. D.J. was born among those peaks in the late 1970s, a naked, one-pound cub in a dark den dug by her mother.

When Thier caught her, D.J. was early in her reproductive years. He estimated she was eight years old and weighed 200 pounds. Thier or U.S. Fish and Wildlife Service biologist Wayne Kasworm would check for D.J.'s radio signal twice a week from an airplane, the Yaak's moody weather permitting. About one of every seven flights they would actually catch a glimpse of her moving through the trees or crossing a talus slope or alpine ridge. They mapped D.J.'s home range of about 100 square miles.

Trappers trapped D.J. when they needed to replace the batteries in her radio collar, capturing her in 1986, 1987, 1990, 1992, 1995, and 1998. At first she was a sucker for bait, but she grew more difficult to capture. Over the years, she topped 320 pounds and perhaps weighed even more when she was fat for hibernation.

D.J.'s year would go like this: Around the first of May she would emerge from a den high on Roderick Mountain. She would descend to eat new grass and sedges on the sunny south-facing slopes and along creek bottoms. In June, she would eat greenery like glacier lilies, biscuitroot, and cow parsnip. In summer, she would sniff out ants and bees and then turn to huckleberries, serviceberries, buffalo berries, and mountain ash berries as the fruits ripened. In fall, she might luck into a gutpile of a moose or elk that a hunter had killed. By mid-November, she would retreat to the high country, digging a new den for the winter.

Most springs, D.J. had cubs in tow. If not, males would smell her mating-season pheromones and come courting in the early summer. At least four males courted D.J.

In the thirteen years D.J. was observed, she produced thirteen cubs. Researchers caught and named Virginia; the triplets
Wade, Fred and Marie; twin brothers Jake and Elwood; twin
sisters Bonnie and Anne; and another set of twins, Maggie and
Seger. D.J. had three other cubs that researchers never captured and thus never named.

Thier particularly recalls the years D. J. had the triplets. By
that time, he had caught D. J. several times and she was growing wise. The second summer D.J. had the triplets, Thier landed
two of the yearlings in snares. Thier could tell by the radio
signal that D.J. was still running loose with the third yearling.
Thier and another trapper loaded shotguns and crept into the
thicket to check the condition of the trapped bears.

"I heard a crashing in the bushes and here comes D.J., just
flying at me. Her ears were up and she was all stiff-legged,"
Thier said. "I thought, 'oh man, this is not good',"

From her posture, Thier figured D.J. was bluffing. In a split
second he decided to call her bluff. He didn't even aim his
shotgun at her. Rather, he waved a fist and shouted: *Get back!*

Fortunately for both of them, D.J. backed off. Thier backed
off, too. He went to town and telephoned for backup. The next
morning, the reinforced trapping team waited nervously for
D.J. to move away from the traps. Finally, the team of trappers
dashed in, fit the yearlings with radios, and set them free.

"Just as we finished, we could hear D.J.'s signal getting stronger," Thier said. "She was coming back for her cubs. It was
almost like she knew the routine and was giving us time to get
our job done. I really feel she gave me a big break that day,"

D.J. reunited with those cubs. But of D.J.'s thirteen known
offspring, only about half survived to adulthood. That's average for grizzly bears and it illustrates why these slow-growing,
slow-breeding animals are easy to exterminate. There are only
a couple of dozen bears in the endangered Yaak population

and D.J. is their grand matriarch. At times, about half the known grizzly bears in the Yaak were her direct descendants. If the Yaak grizzlies can be saved from extinction, it will be in no small part due to D.J.

*   *   *

D.J. DID NOT HAVE HER HOME RANGE all to herself. She lived in relatively remote country, but people were around. And she knew people meant trouble.

"She was certainly seen by people, but they rarely got a good look at her," recalled Kasworm. "Whenever she sensed people, she was on her way. She avoided them, for the most part"

For the most part. But for all her efforts, D.J. couldn't avoid people all the time. Stories about this mother grizzly filtered through the Yaak Valley like woodsmoke through a hemlock forest.

There was, for example, the story of the couple who lived along the Yaak River near the old mining village of Sylvanite. The couple had a small house on a cleared woodlot. One summer the couple adopted a white-tailed deer fawn. Perhaps a car or a mountain lion had killed the doe. The couple hand-raised the fawn, bottle-feeding it until it bonded with its human caretakers as if they were its mother. The spotted fawn followed the couple by day and slept in a fenced enclosure at night. The arrangement was entirely illegal. One may not "adopt" wild animals in Montana, but there were few people to enforce the law up the Yaak.

Over the summer, the fawn grew up but remained attached to its human caretakers. It did not appreciate being left alone. At night the people would shut the deer in its cage and go to sleep. The forlorn fawn would bleat and bawl. The people got used to it.

The fawn's noise became routine. Then one night the couple

heard a different commotion in the yard. There was something out there besides the fawn. Something big.

The couple got out of bed and flicked on the porch lights. Outside, they saw not one but two full-grown grizzly bears eyeing the caged fawn with obvious intent. Together, the bears weighed a half a ton. The little fawn had lured two of the largest meat-eaters in the woods.

The couple slapped their hands and shouted. The bears turned their glowing eyes toward the house. The bears immediately dropped their plans for a midnight snack and fled. Kasworm heard the story and checked the locations of radio-collared grizzly bears. Apparently D.J. was roaming the neighborhood, and since it was mating season, she had evidently attracted a suitor. A state game warden later confiscated the fawn.

• • •

THE SUMMER OF 1994 brought lightning storms and forest fires to the Yaak. The blazes burned until the fall rains snuffed them. The forested slopes became a quilt of blackened, burned woods and green stands that escaped the fires for another year. Fire is a natural component of the landscape and many organisms thrive in its ashes. For example, the heat of forest fires pops open lodgepole pine cones like popcorn kernels, spilling seeds. Another organism marvelously adapted to fire is the morel mushroom.

Wrinkled and gray, the morel looks something like a small brain on a fleshy stem. Though unappealing in looks, it tastes delicious. So delicious, in fact, they are valuable in specialty shops and restaurants. Morels sprout abundantly in the ashes of forest fires and are pursued every summer by nomadic bands of mushroom pickers who sell buckets of the fungi at makeshift trading posts. Humans like morels sautéed in butter with garlic. Grizzly bears are fond of them raw.

The year after forest fire scorched the slopes of D.J.'s home range, the woods sprouted with morel mushrooms. A particularly ambitious mushroom picker ventured deep up Burnt Creek, looking for the motherlode of morels that other pickers had passed by. He found the fungi in abundance. He hunched over and picked as fast as he could, hitting one morel patch, then another.

Absorbed in his work, the picker failed to notice something nearby. Eventually he looked up and saw two small bear cubs a few yards away.

He looked around and, *oh shit*, there was D.J. The picker was caught squarely between a mother grizzly and her two cubs. Of all the types of bear encounters, this may be the most dangerous. The moment the picker noticed D.J., the bear locked eyes on him.

The picker was unarmed, not even carrying a can of pepper spray. He had enough presence of mind not to run. Instead, he flopped onto his belly and covered his head. This was the moment he would live or die.

He could hear D.J. coming fast. The bear rushed in and the picker braced for an attack. Instead, D.J. walked in circles around the picker, huffing and snorting. He could feel her warm, moist exhale on the naked skin of his neck. Finally the bear put those long, strong claws to use. D.J. started ripping up a log a few feet from the prone and cowering man. He heard her tearing into the half-rotten, half-burned tree trunk.

Then the woods went silent. The picker sighed a sigh of very sincere relief. He uncovered his head and looked about. From the ground, the coast looked clear. He stood up.

But no, the grizzlies were still there. D.J. took another look at the picker and charged. Once again, the picker flopped flat on the ground.

The bear had the fellow, you might say, dead to rights. He

was utterly at the animal's mercy. But instead of attacking the man, D.J. once again attacked the log. She ripped into the wood, sending up another shower of bark and wood chips. The bear made an awful ruckus—sending a clear message—but she left the picker unhurt.

This time the picker remained prone for a good, long time. When he arose for the second time, D.J. was indeed gone. The picker collected his bucket and hoofed it back to his rig.

One might expect the picker had learned his lesson. But the lure of the dollar is powerful incentive. The next day the picker returned to Burnt Creek. This time he carried a gun. But he had no trouble with D.J. She had wisely taken her cubs elsewhere.

Thier says D.J. could have easily killed the picker, had she wanted to.

"People think bears are monsters. They're not monsters. They're far more tolerant of people than people think they are," Thier said. An unarmed human is no match for a determined bear, but most times a grizzly charges, it is just bluffing.

"I believe it's a conscious choice the bear makes, not to kill people in these cases," Thier said. "There's a lot going on between their ears, a lot more than people give them credit for,"

*   *   *

KASWORM POINTS OUT that D.J.—a shy, retiring, retreating, peaceable, largely vegetarian animal—is very much a typical grizzly. For her entire life, she minded her own business. She lived largely out of sight of humans, although rarely very far from them. She didn't eat garbage or other unnatural foods. She is far more typical to the species Ursus arctos than most of the bears in this book and those that make headlines. It is important to remember that.

In August 1998, Kasworm's trapping team nabbed D.J. one

more time. An examination of her mammary glands indicated she had no cubs. Kasworm figured D.J. might be pregnant and would have cubs in the spring. From an airplane that autumn, Kasworm followed D.J.'s signal to her winter den.

In June 1999, Kasworm flew over the familiar landmarks of D.J.'s home range, eager to pick up her signal as he had for thirteen years. The plane crested the bald summits of Roderick Mountain and Grizzly Peak. Kasworm finally picked up her signal coming from the dense forest of larch and Douglas fir in Seventeenmile Creek. He marked his map and flew home.

When the June rains allowed, Kasworm flew again. He found the radio signal coming from the exact same spot. After a third flight, the signal hadn't moved.

"I thought 'Uh oh, something's going on here. I'm going to have to go take a look.'"

Kasworm figured there was a logical explanation for the immobile radio collar. D.J. lost weight over hibernation and the collar slipped over her ears. It happened all the time. With that in mind, Kasworm drove up the Yaak to Sylvanite, then turned on the one-lane bridge leading to Seventeenmile Creek. When he couldn't drive any farther, he followed the radio signal on foot.

In 1999 D.J. was twenty years old, but Kasworm figured she still had a couple more litters left in her life. At that time Kasworm figured about twenty grizzlies lived in the Yaak and the population was growing. Kasworm was not only following D.J. but now had radio collars on D.J.'s daughters and granddaughters.

"Things looked like they were doing pretty well up the Yaak, largely thanks to D.J.," Kasworm said. "We saw a population that we definitely thought was increasing,"

As Kasworm walked through the forest, he smelled trouble. As the radio signal got louder, the smell of decaying flesh became stronger. Following both signals, Kasworm found D.J. Rather, he found what was left of her.

It was June and D.J. had been dead for a week. Her carcass was largely decomposed. Kasworm picked up her collar and searched for clues. Her bones were scattered, some missing or broken, indicating she had been fed upon.

Kasworm found more. D.J. had indeed given birth to cubs, again twins. Kasworm found their carcasses, also partially consumed. Kasworm next found the bones, hide, and hair of a cow elk, even more decayed than the bear carcasses.

Kasworm looked closely. On the brush near the carcasses, he collected bear hairs, the long guard hairs of an adult bear. But the hairs were dark brown. D.J. was light brown. In the Yaak, male bears tend to be darker than females.

Kasworm tried to piece together the story of D.J.'s final stand. Although he acknowledges it's largely speculation and conjecture, he figures D.J.'s final days went something like this:

After emerging from her winter den with her two young cubs, D.J. descended into the lower elevations of Seventeenmile Creek, looking for food. A cow elk had succumbed to the rigors of winter. D.J. caught a whiff of the carcass, perhaps from a mile away. She followed her nose toward the prize.

A male grizzly was doing the same thing, coming from another direction.

It's unclear which bear found the elk first. Most likely it was D.J., since it seems unlikely a wise mother like D.J. would risk the lives of her cubs by challenging an adult male on a carcass. So imagine D.J. and her cubs feeding on the elk when the adult male barges in, demanding the carcass for himself.

D.J. defended her cubs but was no match for the larger male. Once the male killed D.J., it was a simple matter to finish off the cubs. The male went on to consume not only the elk but D.J. and her cubs as well.

The tale is just one interpretation of a few clues, not scientific fact. But knowing what we do about grizzly bears, it makes a certain degree of sense.

Cannibalism among grizzly bears isn't common, nor is it unheard of. In fact, one of D.J.'s previous offspring had been killed and eaten by another bear in nearby Burnt Creek. When cannibalism occurs, it most often involves cubs killed by adult males. One of the reasons female grizzlies instinctively defend their cubs is because they have always had to defend them against their own species.

The evolutionary "reason" why bears would kill members of their own species is not exactly understood. Biologists speculate that when a male bear destroys the cubs of a another bear, the male may later mate with the female and produce cubs of his own. D.J.'s case is more complicated, since it included competition over the elk carcass and the fact that the male killed the mother bear as well as her cubs. D.J. may have died in a simple dispute over food. "After thirteen years, her death was a big disappointment," Kasworm said. "But in some respects, I'm glad it occurred as a natural event. I knew D.J. was twenty years old and coming to the end of her natural life span."

Then, lest he slip out of his role as objective scientist, Kasworm added: "We were fortunate to obtain thirteen years of data."

* * *

THE LOSS OF D.J. was just the beginning of bad news for the Yaak bears. For ten years, Kasworm had watched the local grizzly population slowly grow. On average, one bear died each year but enough cubs survived to keep the population growing.

Before 1999 was over, another young female was shot in self-defense and an adult male was destroyed after he killed a goat and chickens at rural homes. The next year, Kasworm recorded three cubs that died of natural causes and suspects a poacher killed a young female.

All of a sudden things looked bleak for grizzly bears up the Yaak. Yet Kasworm was still hopeful, even optimistic. D.J.'s offspring, and her offspring's offspring, still roam the deep forests and bald mountaintops of the Yaak. In her twenty years, D.J. had given the population a crucial boost. Her genetic predisposition—reclusive, peaceable, and fecund—is a good pattern to pass on.

While the Yaak grizzly population remains in danger, it's still hanging on. Whether grizzly bears will continue to find a home in the Yaak into the 21st Century depends on the bears' skill at surviving in a world full of humans and on our own will to tolerate a world with bears.

A Legend
in Our Time

BILL MOSHER RODE THE RUGGED BACK FORTY OF HIS CATTLE RANCH, cowboy hat firmly on his head. He was a bit steamed: That day he lost a valuable, 700-pound Angus calf. He found the animal dead of a crushed spine and skull.

Mosher rode the modern equivalent of a trusty steed—a four-wheel-drive all-terrain vehicle. Montana Department of Fish, Wildlife and Parks grizzly bear biologist Mike Madel was on board as well, jouncing uncomfortably as the chubby tires rolled over rocks, ruts, and badger holes.

That autumn day in 1992, Mosher and Madel were along the upper Dearborn River near the Rocky Mountain Front southwest of Augusta. The Front is where the jagged limestone fortress of the Rockies rises above the Great Plains. It's the landscape that inspired A. B. Guthrie's phrase, "Big Sky Country." Here, the mythical Old West meets the modern New West, one boot planted firmly in the past, the other in the present. Mosher and Madel were there to investigate the killing.

Madel studied the kill site like a detective at a crime scene. Madel and Mosher agreed the evidence pointed toward a large, male grizzly. Madel pieced the story together: The herd of cows and their nearly grown calves were feeding in a forest of lodgepole pine. The bear approached over a small rise, walking directly toward the stock until they started to spook. Then the bear burst into a full charge. Cattle panicked in all directions. In its dim-minded confusion, one calf plowed into a tree. The bear was on the calf in a split second, biting it severely in the back where the neck joins the shoulders. The bear ate the calf's entrails, the fat over the sternum, and the muscle tissue from the hindquarters.

After investigating the scene, Madel and federal Animal Damage Control trapper Jim Stevens set foot snares around the partially eaten carcass. Toward evening, Mosher and Madel returned toward ranch headquarters. Mosher steered the four-wheeler along a creek bottom lined with aspen and fir trees. Suddenly Mosher squeezed the brakes and skidded to a halt.

Ahead of them was the bear, sprinting away in high gear. At a glance Madel figured the animal was a male weighing perhaps 700 pounds. The bear was in its autumn prime. Its glossy, chocolate-brown coat rippled over a muscular black hump. Powerful hindquarters launched the bear up the open slope at full tilt. The bear's power brought to Madel's mind the image of a locomotive. Now and again the bear looked over its shoulder to see if these dangerous humans were pursuing it.

"He ran like he expected us to start shooting at him at any moment. You could almost read the expression on his face," Madel said. "It was like '*Uh oh, they almost caught me.*'"

That was one of Madel's few glimpses of the Falls Creek grizzly in the wild. The grizzly was just one of scores of bears that live along the Rocky Mountain Front, but that particular bear occupied the thoughts—and chipped away at the pocketbooks—of cattlemen, biologists, and trappers for a full fifteen years.

* * *

THE HISTORY of the American West is full of "notorious" or "renegade" stock-killing bears, a segment of history that seems scripted from Louis L'Amour novels. Details varied from Colorado's San Juan Mountains to Utah's Wasatch Front to the Idaho Sawtooths, but the basic plot was the same. It went like this: A bear would be caught by a steel leg-hold trap but would escape to earn nicknames like Old Two Toes, Old Three Toes, Old Club Foot, Old Three-Legs. These cagey bears grew fat off livestock, leaving their distinctive tracks around the kills. Cattlemen found the kills, cursed their luck, and put a reward on the bear's head. Meanwhile, the bear displayed a supernatural ability to foil trappers and frustrate hunters, and sometimes left a trail of maimed or dead people in its wake.

Eventually a righteous, clean-living fellow would vow to hunt down the beast, like St. George slaying a dragon. Lured by reward money and a desire to make the world a better place, the hunter ventured alone into the wilderness. After enduring storms, rockfalls, and other mountain hazards, the hunter faced the bear and brought justice to it in a blaze of gunfire. Once killed, these bears tended to weigh in excess of 1,000 pounds, although certified scales were rarely within riding distance.

Frontier Montana had its share of legendary stock-killers. In the 1890s, a grizzly named Two Toes roamed the Mission Mountains, the Swan Range, and the Swan Valley in between. (This was an entirely different Two Toes than the bear that killed John Graham and Frank Welch in the Yellowstone country in the early 20th Century.) Two Toes reportedly gobbled down a small fortune in livestock before it was hunted down.

A grizzly dubbed Old Terror roamed the Cabinet Mountains around 1900. The bear reportedly killed twenty hogs in one night at a homestead near Troy. One hunter reported firing sixteen shots at the bear at close range, while another fired twenty-three shots even closer. Journalists of the day credited the bear's survival to its supernatural toughness, rather than the hunters' poor marksmanship. Eventually, though, even Old

Terror lost his mojo and was captured in a steel trap.

In an earlier time, the Falls Creek grizzly could have become a similar legend: a full-blown, rip-snortin' skull-smashin' renegade, come down from the mountains to deliver holy hell on honest ranchers. But times had changed...or had they?

. . .

THE FIRST PERSON to write of the Rocky Mountain Front near Falls Creek was explorer Meriwether Lewis, who split from his partner William Clark to explore this country in July 1806. Lewis crossed the Rockies from the west on an old Nez Perce hunting route, emerging onto the Great Plains a couple of miles south of Falls Creek Ridge. Lewis found the mountains full of passenger pigeons and the prairies crowded with bison. Today, the pigeons are extinct and the bison were nearly exterminated. But the Rocky Mountain Front was grizzly country then, and it's grizzly country today.

Across the West, the historic pattern was to simply exterminate grizzly bears in places where we grazed sheep and cattle. This was the way from Kansas to California, New Mexico to North Dakota. But in the 1920s, Montana set a different goal: Try somehow to conserve grizzly bears while raising livestock on the same landscape.

Today, Mike Madel's job is to help smooth the sometimes rocky relations between the Front's ranchers and its grizzly bears. In essence, Madel is a problem-solver. When a bear smashes up commercial beehives, Madel helps the beekeeper erect an electric fence around the remaining hives to prevent a repeat performance. When livestock die naturally, say during spring calving season, Madel's department collects the carcasses and takes them into remote areas away from ranches.

Most grizzly bears, Madel says, do not kill livestock. They have plenty of other, safer foods to eat. However, when individual grizzlies do make a habit of killing stock, they become expensive problems for ranchers, especially those raising sheep.

"Once they start killing sheep, it's very difficult to get a bear to stop," Madel said. "It's different with cattle. With cattle, there's substantial risk involved for the bear. Mother cows are good at protecting calves. I've watched cows rush toward both bears and wolves, driving them away from their calves."

Imagine you're a young, 150-pound grizzly, away from your mother for the first time. Curious, you approach a cow and calf. Suddenly, the half-ton beast charges toward you, looking all the world like she'll kick your fuzzy fanny back to the mountains. Most bears do that once or twice and learn to leave cows alone.

In a surprising way, bears today depend on the open space guaranteed by cattle ranching. If ranchers go belly-up, they may sell their land for subdivisions. Even with their temptations and dangers, ranches are far better for wildlife than subdivisions. And many ranchers don't mind having a few grizzlies around. What they can't afford is feeding bears that make a habit of eating their livestock.

•   •   •

IN THE 1970s AND '80s, biologist Keith Aune conducted radio telemetry research on grizzlies along the Rocky Mountain Front. It was cutting-edge science, learning about bears' habits in an area primarily dedicated to ranching and farming. Aune needed to catch bears to outfit them with radio collars. He set foot snares on Bill Mosher's ranch, where the mountains turn to prairie.

In May 1985, Aune knew there was a pair of grizzlies—a male and female—near Cuniff Creek. It was breeding season, and the two were traveling together. Aune carefully hid a foot snare baited with a pile of meat in a patch of aspen trees. The male investigated the bait and carefully uncovered a small piece of the cable. With that, the bear stayed away. Aune knew he was working with a cagey bear.

The female, however, was not as cautious. Aune nabbed her in a foot snare. She was three years old and became another subject of Aune's research.

Aune still wanted the male, but the bruin simply wouldn't fall for traditional bait. The female had urinated on the ground where she had been caught, so Aune collected that mud and wadded it into a ball. He then dug a small hole and placed a snare inside it. He baited that hole with the mud ball saturated with the scent of the female, full of the powerful pheromones of mating season.

When Aune later checked his trap, he found a six-year-old male grizzly securely held by the snare. Aune put a radio collar on the bear, took measurements, and tattooed identification numbers on the bear's gum. The male received the number 346. Later, he would be known as the Falls Creek grizzly.

Those bears did kill cattle, especially the female. Three times state wildlife biologists caught her after she killed cattle on prairie ranches. Three times they hauled her into the mountains and set her free. Each time she returned and killed more livestock. Finally she killed more animals than local ranchers could tolerate, and a Montana hunter killed her in a tightly supervised depredation hunt.

The male killed cattle occasionally. Madel suspects he picked up the habit from the female. No. 346's home range stretched over 175 square miles around a prominent, north-south escarpment called Falls Creek Ridge. Mostly, the Falls Creek male stayed in the mountains, deep within the Scapegoat Wilderness of the Lewis and Clark National Forest. He spent his summers on high mountain slopes, feeding on biscuitroot and other nutritious plants. He stayed away from people, with all their noise, stink, and pesky traps.

By autumn 1985, No. 346 slipped his radio collar. Wildlife authorities could not follow his day-to-day activities, but they still heard from the bear. Every so often a rancher found the remains of a calf or yearling that had been killed by a bear and called Madel.

Madel knew the tracks of No. 346 were six-and-a-quarter inches across the front pad. "I measured his tracks many, many times," Madel said. "I mean hundreds of tracks. It's not like he killed calves every year, but every other year or so I would get another call. I would go check it out and find his tracks."

"We lose three or four calves a year to documented grizzly kills on the Rocky Mountain Front, south of the Blackfeet Reservation," Madel said. But that's over 1,800 square miles of rangeland, including thousands of cattle.

In this area a pattern emerged. When a rancher found a fresh kill, he would call the Montana Department of Fish, Wildlife and Parks and a trapper from the federal Animal Damage Control. Trappers from the two agencies jointly investigated the kill site. If they agreed a grizzly made the kill, they would set snares or culvert traps. Other grizzlies got caught, but bear No. 346 would sniff the troubling scent of humans and leave the trap sets alone.

In 1988 Madel figured the Falls Creek male killed two yearlings and a calf. But for the next three years, ranchers reported no losses that could be attributed to that particular bear. In 1992 a yearling and a calf were killed. In both cases, the clues matched the Falls Creek male's mode of operation, track size, and home range.

In the fall cattle roundup of 1993, Bill Mosher ended up short nine calves. Mosher believed the Falls Creek male killed them, although there was no direct evidence. Even so, Madel agrees the calves were probably killed and eaten by No. 346.

In 1994 and 1995 there were no reports of missing live-

152 - Great Montana Bear Stories

stock from the bear's home range. One calf was killed in 1996, but the bear tracks were too small to match the Falls Creek male.

Things heated up in 1997. Five calves were killed in the Falls Creek drainage, and evidence pointed vaguely toward No. 346. In 1998, two yearlings were killed in the same drainage, but in 1999 and 2000 no stock was reported missing. The bear may have killed calves that ranchers didn't know about, but that's his record according to the evidence, Madel said.

Newspaper reporters picked up the story of the Falls Creek grizzly. Among the best was Scott McMillion of the Bozeman *Daily Chronicle*. McMillion put the bear's mass into scale: The bear stood nine feet high and weighed more than 650 pounds. McMillion noted the bear was two feet taller than National Basketball Association giant Shaquille O'Neil, weighed twice as much, and was much, much faster.

Tim Tew, manager of the LF Ranch, told another newspaper reporter he figured the bear cost him thousands of dollars a year in lost beef, over 13 years. Bill Mosher told a reporter he had lost at least one cow and 20 calves to the bruin over the years. The private conservation group Defenders of Wildlife reimbursed ranchers for stock lost to bears, which helped take some of the sting out of the depredations.

For more than a decade, the Falls Creek grizzly conducted his hit-and-run calf kills. One official from the U.S. Department of Agriculture credited the Falls Creek bear with killing some $200,000 worth of beef. Madel disputes that figure as overblown, saying No. 346 was credited with calves that may have been killed by wolves, cougars, black bears, coyotes, or other grizzly bears. Some of the alleged kills may have been animals that died of harsh weather or natural causes and were simply scavenged by the bear.

Looking at the evidence, Madel figures the Falls Creek male killed twenty-one calves, five yearlings, and one cow. If all those animals made it to market, their total value would be about $16,600. That's no small loss, but it's less than one-tenth of the figure trumpeted by the Agriculture Department.

Nonetheless, once the inflated $200,000 figure made the newspapers, it stuck. It was repeated in magazine and press accounts just like that 1900-era Cabinet Range grizzly that magically absorbed nearly forty bullets without harm. The Falls Creek grizzly was larger than life.

"What transpired here was a story," said Aune. "That bear became mythologized. That bear became *the* bear of that country. People lost sight of the fact that there were other bears in that country, including other big males that we know occasionally killed livestock. Everything got pinned on 346. In the mythology, the Falls Creek male was the biggest, oldest bear in the Rocky Mountain Front, neither of which was true."

* * *

SINCE THE BEAR WAS PROTECTED under the Endangered Species Act, trappers could not pursue the bear on the Lewis and Clark National Forest. But whenever the bear killed on a private ranch, trappers did their best to nab him. They never did.

"The most astounding thing about him was that he was just so darn elusive," Madel said. "Even in those early years, we just couldn't catch him. There were many, many attempts. Whenever anyone would move onto a kill site, the bear would just leave and not return."

Madel remembers one typical case in July 1988. A rancher found a freshly killed calf in a rugged portion of his ranch. The tracks matched 346. The rancher had not disturbed the kill in any way. Madel figured this was his chance.

Wearing scent-free rubber boots and rubber gloves, Madel set his snares very carefully, burying them lightly with duff. He backed away thinking, *This is a good set.*

The next morning, there was a bear in the trap, but it was a big black bear. Madel looked around and, sure enough, found grizzly tracks. The Falls Creek male had evidently returned to the kill site, found the upset black bear in the trap, and walked a wide circle about it. For all his careful work, Madel had succeeded only in teaching No. 346 another lesson.

Few people ever saw the bear. In September 1992, a bowhunter was looking for elk near Cuniff Creek. Stalking through the hills, he walked onto a big, chocolate grizzly feasting on a freshly killed calf. Trappers responded, but of course by then the bear was long gone.

•   •   •

By 2001 the Falls Creek grizzly was about twenty-two years old. He was growing bolder, or perhaps less wary. That April cows were giving birth on the LF Ranch. Even though it was nearly Easter, snow covered the ground and bitter winds blew off the mountains. Manager Tim Tew herded the pregnant cows into the protection of a cottonwood creek bottom. The calving odors attracted scavengers—including a few bears.

On Good Friday morning, Tew found three dead calves. He found another the next day. Big grizzly tracks were pressed into the mud. The cattle were so frightened they would not stay in the cottonwood bottom, instead remaining on exposed slopes where newborn calves risked hypothermia. The LF Ranch is considerably north of the Falls Creek bear's normal range, so No. 346 was not considered the chief suspect.

Tew called for help from Madel and federal Animal Damage Control trappers. It's illegal for a rancher to kill a grizzly, so Madel gave Tew some shotgun shells loaded with harmless but noisy firecrackers. As Tew drove a county road on the ranch, he saw a big, dark-brown bear staring at a cow and its bawling calf. Tew scrambled out of his truck and shouted at the bear, which stood about fifty yards away. The bear didn't retreat. Tew blasted two cracker shells at the bear, but it didn't leave until Tew fired a third round.

On Easter Sunday, Madel and others set two foot snares and a culvert trap on the LF Ranch. The bear ignored the traps— but killed two more calves by Monday. Trappers set more snares but to no avail.

Bears weren't the only predators giving Tew headaches that season. Coyotes had been hanging around the birthing area as well, dashing among the cows to snatch a calf. Animal Damage Control agents responded by shooting coyotes from a helicopter. While looking for coyotes, the gunner and pilot spotted the tracks of a grizzly. The tracks led into a ridge thick with pine and aspen, but didn't lead out. The bear was holed up in the thick cover.

The gunner traded his shotgun for a dart gun loaded with immobilizing drugs. While Madel waited on the ground, the federal pilot skimmed low over the piney ridge. The gunner spotted the bear and fired as the helicopter swooped low. The dart struck the bear in the rump, and the bear sagged into unconsciousness.

Madel and others scrambled to the scene. Cautiously they approached the hulking mass of the downed bear. They gave the bear another shot of immobilizing drug. Madel lifted the bear's lip: Faintly visible on the gum was the number Keith Aune had tattooed fifteen years before, 346. The Falls Creek male was finally in hand.

No. 346 weighed 595 pounds, about 150 pounds less than he would weigh at his autumn peak. His muzzle and forehead bore scars from battles with rival males. The bear was well past his prime. The canines that had once crushed the spines of yearling cattle were worn to dull nubs. His molars were pitted with decay. It was becoming increasingly difficult for him to survive, leading him to take his chances in the ranch lands. A tender young calf was just the meal for his worn-out teeth.

Tim Tew and others chained three four-wheelers together to generate enough horsepower to haul the drugged bear out of the thicket through the deep snow. From there, they hoisted the massive animal into a steel culvert trap. The gate shut with a clang. It signaled the end of an era.

"There was a change, both in his movements and in his wariness around people," Madel said, recounting the differences. The bear had stood his ground against Tew instead of fleeing in near panic as it had fled Madel and Mosher years before. The bear usually spent most of its year in the mountains, but now it ventured far onto the prairie ranch lands. In previous years the bear hit-and-ran when it killed a calf; now it lingered on a ranch and killed repeatedly, in spite of all the human activity around it.

A complex set of rules dictates when wildlife authorities may destroy grizzly bears. This time, officials figured No. 346's cost to the local ranching community outweighed what it might contribute biologically to the local bear population. Truth be told, No. 346 was running out of time regardless of what people did. He had lived a long life.

There was no final volley of bullets, no last valiant charge for Bear No. 346. Instead, Madel hitched the culvert trap to his pickup truck and drove south to Bozeman where Keith Aune, the researcher who first caught the bear in 1985, was waiting for him. Aune was head of the state's wildlife laboratory. He would be the one to finish the job.

On the drive south, No. 346 roused from the drugs. At the laboratory it was necessary to poke a jab stick into the trap and immobilize the bear again. Then Aune used an electric clipper to shave a patch of the great bear's foreleg, exposing a vein. Using a hypodermic needle the size of a tube of toothpaste,

Aune gave the great bear one last injection, watching as the animal breathed its last.

When the bear was dead, newspaper reporters interviewed the ranchers. To a man, they said it was time for No. 346 to be destroyed. But they also said a part of them would miss the old cuss. "It's kind of sad," Tew said. "That old bugger's been around a long time."

In the old days, grizzlies were exterminated, not conserved. Times had changed. Yet the human tendency to seek out a single culprit for a complex problem had not changed.

"It seems human nature to want to find someone to take the blame," Aune said. "People think we can fix the problem simply by removing one bear. The truth is that when we pin the problems of cattle depredation on a single animal, we lose sight of the bigger picture of what is happening on the land. We miss the real message here. Some bears that have the opportunity to kill cows will take advantage of the opportunity. Killing one bear doesn't erase that picture.

"This idea that we are going to totally eliminate conflicts is just inappropriate. It's just not going to happen. As long as we engage in human activity in grizzly bear habitat, there will be conflicts. We can minimize and mitigate conflicts, but that's about it. Of course, it's easy for me to say that. I don't have a lot of cows grazing in grizzly country on the Rocky Mountain Front."

One of Montana's most famous stock-killers was not a bear at all. It was a wolf. Specifically, it was the Custer wolf, which disemboweled cattle of the Judith Basin country in the 1930s. Local librarian Elva Wiseman wrote melodramas about the Custer wolf that were published around the country. The Custer wolf gained mythic proportions, but it was just a wolf and was eventually hunted down. Today, the Custer wolf stands stuffed at the courthouse in Stanford.

Almost as an epithet, Wiseman wrote of the Custer Wolf: "He was a killer, but he was a gallant animal, one to make your blood pressure mount a bit higher. He gave us food for speculation for fifteen years as we bet on and against him. It's been awful quiet in the basin since he's been gone."

The same could be said for the Falls Creek grizzly. Word for word.

A Hunter, an Elk, and a Grizzly

Timothy "Omar" Hilston was born in Ohio and adopted Montana as his home with his characteristic joy and enthusiasm. Hilston served in the Air Force at Malmstrom Air Force Base near Great Falls. After leaving the military, Hilston insisted on returning to Montana. In 2001, he worked as an X-ray service engineer and spent every free weekend in the mountains. He was a friendly guy, with a ready grin and a playful streak. He loved his family. He loved the mountains. He loved the wildlife. In particular, he loved hunting.

Even before the 2001 hunting season opened, Hilston enjoyed a stroke of good fortune. He was one of fifty hunters to draw a coveted "Boyd Mountain tag" allowing him to hunt the Blackfoot-Clearwater Game Range. The range is 67,000 acres of ponderosa pine forest and grasslands managed by the Montana Department of Fish, Wildlife and Parks. It is just north of U.S. Highway 200, about one hundred miles west of Great Falls and forty miles east of Missoula. The terrain is rolling, gentle foothills, backed up against the towering ramparts of the Bob Marshall Wilderness. Hunting here is a rare treat.

Hilston left his home in Great Falls at four-thirty in the morning of October 30, stopping at Wal-Mart for a few last odds-and-ends. He pointed his pickup truck west and drove over the Continental Divide. He arrived at the game range shortly before dawn and drove a couple of miles into the forest. Hilston and his grown daughter had hunted here the weekend before and discovered a herd of 200 elk. He had a strategy sketched out in his mind and couldn't wait to get back after them. Although Hilston ventured into the backcountry with friends and family as often as he could, he was confident and skilled enough to hunt alone.

Hilston found a place to leave his pickup. There he quietly collected his gear, loaded his rifle, and stepped into the morning gloaming. The forest was open ponderosa pine with a carpet of pine grass and fallen needles. It bordered a large meadow where elk fed in the cover of night. After the fall rains, hunting was as quiet as walking in stocking feet. Since it was midweek, the refuge was not at all crowded. Given his hunting style, Hilston probably crept down to the edge of the big meadow and glassed for elk. It was the last sunrise Hilston would ever see.

•   •   •

ABOUT THAT SAME TIME—daybreak—Tom Sidor awoke back in Great Falls. Sidor was Hilston's brother-in-law and an avid hunter himself. Hilston had asked Sidor to go with him that day, but Sidor had to turn him down. He had business in Missoula and couldn't afford the time off work. Sidor did promise he would stop by the game range on his way to Missoula to see if Hilston had found an elk. Both men knew the odds were good that Hilston would fill an elk tag that day.

Sidor arrived at the game range about nine-thirty that morning. Following Hilston's directions he found Hilston's pickup just where he expected it. He thought Hilston might be there, smiling as usual, perhaps with a new hunting story to tell. Sidor had a packboard, boots, and gear in his car and was ready to help butcher and carry out meat if Hilston had an elk down. But the truck was empty. Hilston was nowhere to be found.

Sidor wasn't worried. Not yet, anyway. It was only mid-morning. The day was young. Sidor waited the rest of the morning for Hilston to return to his pickup truck. At one-thirty in the afternoon, Sidor scribbled a note on the back of a business card and jammed it under Hilston's windshield wiper. Then he continued to Missoula. He figured Hilston would be okay; Omar was the kind of super-prepared hunter who carried two flashlights in his daypack.

"I thought, obviously, he has taken one heck of a hike here," Sidor said. "But even at that point, it didn't set right. He knew I was coming to meet him. It was just a question of whether I would show up at nine-fifteen or nine-forty five."

Throughout the day, Sidor tried Hilston's cell phone. He called Hilston's wife, Mary Ann, back in Great Falls. She hadn't heard from him. Sidor checked into a Missoula motel, and as evening turned into night, he returned to the game range.

Sidor found Hilston's pickup with his note still plastered to the glass. The gear inside the cab hadn't been touched. Now worrisome thoughts began to creep into Sidor's imagination. The night was inky black with low clouds. It was starting to drizzle. Sidor trusted Hilston's woodsmanship, but knew he wasn't the kind of guy to totally blow off a rendezvous. Sidor honked his car horn and flashed his headlights but got no response.

Using his cell phone, Sidor called Hilston's wife. She still had no word from her husband and was worried. The deserted pickup didn't feel right to Sidor. A nagging hunch told him something was wrong, even if he couldn't figure out exactly what. He dialed 9-1-1 and punched "send."

*   *   *

Sidor spent the night at Hilston's pickup. Daylight came Wednesday morning but brought no sign of the hunter. The sheriff, his deputies, and the volunteer search-and-rescue team gathered and began combing the woods. The going was easy: The terrain was nearly flat and the forest was open.

The search team included a German shepherd and trainer. It was the dog that first found sign. But it wasn't direct sign of Hilston but rather the blood trail of an elk, only a few hundred yards from Hilston's truck. Nose to the duff, the dog charged through the woods.

At the end of the trail the dog found the fresh carcass of a cow elk buried under a gnarled and scarred aspen tree. Animals had obviously eaten a portion of the animal and cached the rest under a layer of dirt and pine needles. But the odd thing was, one of the elk's legs was tied to a tree with a length of twine.

Then the searchers found a .270 rifle on the ground about twelve feet from the elk. Two live rounds were in the magazine, and the bolt was open on an empty chamber. It was Hilston's gun.

It was the first time anyone in the search party had seriously considered Hilston had run into bear trouble. "It didn't cross our minds," Sidor said. "No one anticipated it was a bear issue until that point. Frankly, I didn't either."

The discovery immediately changed the search. The team started a new pattern, using the dead elk as the center. About 100 yards away they found the tattered body of Omar Hilston.

It appeared Hilston was the first hunter to be killed by a grizzly bear in Montana in nearly fifty years. News of the attack blazed across the state's newspapers. Wildlife officials immediately closed the game range and called all forty-nine remaining holders of the area's elk permits. The hunters would have to stay home while state and federal agencies conducted a hunt of their own. The search for Hilston was over. The search for an explanation had just begun.

*   *   *

HILSTON'S DEATH WAS SHOCKING in part because it was so unusual. Hunters die every year in Montana, but the activity is still correctly considered very safe. Typical risks include icy roads, hypothermia, and sloppy gun handling. In the past half-century in Montana, only two hunters have been killed by bears.

In 1956, the tiny central Montana town of Loma was the home of a 29-year-old farmer and former high school sports star named Kenneth Scott. That fall Scott and friends hunted elk south of Marias Pass on the Lewis and Clark National Forest. According to newspaper accounts, Scott and another hunter named Squires surprised a grizzly, which charged. Squires backed away from the bear but tripped and fell. The bear bit and clawed at his logging boot.

Scott fired two rounds into the bear, which retreated into thick brush. The men decided to track the bear and finish it off. This was no small act of bravery, as Scott was armed only with a lever-action 30-30 rifle, a relatively light bear gun. Scott found the bear at very close range and fired four more rounds at it. The wounded bear attacked again, this time badly mauling Scott. Scott died hours later from his injuries, perhaps compounded by hypothermia. His hunting party later finished off the bear.

Other Montana hunters have been injured—but not fatally—by grizzlies.

In September 2001, a grizzly mauled an archery hunter in the Madison Range after evidently being drawn to the sound of the hunter's elk bugle and the smell of his bottled elk scent. Another not-exactly-uncommon occurrence is when a quiet hunter surprises a bear in a daybed or on a trail. Grizzlies, particularly mother bears with cubs, will sometimes attack in these close encounters. When a bear does attack, it most often leaves the human bleeding but able to walk out.

Twice since the 1980s, Montana pheasant hunters have been charged by grizzlies when their dogs flushed bears instead of birds. In one case near Choteau, the bear injured the hunter and ran off. In the other, in the Mission Valley near Ronan, the hunter shot the bear as the animal ran headlong into him. The bear died but slammed into the hunter so hard it bent the steel barrel of his 12-gauge shotgun.

Surprise encounters and harassing bird dogs are one thing. Hilston's death was something else again.

* * *

INVESTIGATORS PIECED TOGETHER the few clues of Hilston's final hunt and created this theory of the attack:

Hilston found elk that morning and shot a cow. The shot was well placed and the elk crashed away only a short distance before crumpling at the base of an aspen. Hilston must have smiled at the ironic twists of elk hunting: Sometimes it's hard and sometimes it's easy. This time, well, he was only 400 yards from his truck.

Hilston laid down his rifle; it had done its job. Then Hilston punched the date on his elk tag as required by law. He used logger's ribbon to flag a trail to a point where he could see his pickup. He used a lot of ribbon, perhaps as a signal for Sidor.

Then the hard work started. Hilston rolled the elk on its back and tied a hind leg to a tree so it wouldn't roll back. He set to work. Gutting an elk is a bent-over, head down, muscle-straining job that demands attention. Hilston had just begun. He probably never saw death coming.

The bear came in fast, probably as Hilston was hunched over his elk. Hilston didn't carry bear pepper spray and probably wouldn't have had time to use it anyway.

The bear swarmed in, swatting and biting, in an attack that was as brief as it was ferocious. Hilston was demobilized in seconds, and the bear turned its focus to eating and burying the elk. The injured Hilston regained his feet and struggled toward his pickup. He made it about halfway before he died.

*   *   *

INVESTIGATORS FOUND TRACKS of an adult grizzly at the elk carcass and smaller bear tracks on ground squirrel mounds nearby, indicating a female with cubs. The most sinister theory is that the female bear saw Hilston standing over the elk, charged in and simply removed him as competition for food.

Montana Department of Fish, Wildlife and Parks bear specialist James Jonkel suspects otherwise. He suggests the eager, hungry, and foolish cubs may have rushed in first and then the sow charged to defend them after realizing there was a human on the elk.

FWP bear researcher Rick Mace proposed another hypothesis: That the bear might not have distinguished the man from the elk until it was too late. After all, the air was full of elk scent and blood, and Hilston was probably bent over, straddling the carcass. The female bear may have rushed in fast, thinking it was going to finish off a wounded elk and not even realizing there was a man present until it was too late to avoid a confrontation.

"That's just as likely as any other scenario," Mace said. "We'll never know for sure. You can't know what goes on in an animal's head."

Mace said one of the most important things about Hilston's death is not blowing it out of proportion. "We have to keep this in perspective. We have to take it seriously, but one death in fifty years does not make any sort of trend."

In Montana, hunters collectively spend 2.5 million days

afield every year. They are much more likely to be shot dead by one of their Brothers in Orange than be killed by a bear. Since the 1950s, only two Montana hunters have been killed by bears but more than 100 hunters have been fatally shot by themselves or other hunters.

Warden Jeff Campbell was among the first to investigate Hilston scene. "He did everything right, as far as I could tell," he said. "He was just at the wrong place at the wrong time."

* * *

HILSTON'S DEATH BRINGS UP the unsettling phenomenon of "dinnerbell bears." That is, some grizzly bears evidently have learned to associate the sound of gunfire with the opportunity for a free meal. Campfire tales tell of bears that trot to elk kills like a house cat coming to the sound of an electric can opener. Bears have followed pack strings loaded with elk quarters. In one documented case outside Yellowstone, two Wyoming hunters were dragging a deer out of the woods when they felt a strange tug in the opposite direction. They turned to find a grizzly bear pulling on the other end of the deer. In that case, the bear ended up dead.

Jonkel believes some bears do learn to associate the sound of a gunshot with a free gut pile. "These are not stupid animals," Jonkel said. "Some bears know when hunting season is coming, just as they know when huckleberries ripen or when salmon run in spawning streams."

In September 2000, Jonkel trapped a young grizzly in the Blackfoot area that had learned to associate bow hunters' tree stands with a meal of white-tailed deer. That bear followed bow hunters to their stands and waited nearby for them to kill something. Understandably, this frightened the bow hunters. Eventually, officials destroyed that bear.

Nonetheless, Jonkel called the Hilston attack "very strange."

It certainly was almost freakishly unusual, but it isn't unheard of. In 1995, two hunters in British Columbia suffered a hauntingly similar fate. In that case, the hunters likewise failed to return from a hunting trip. Searchers in a helicopter spotted a female grizzly with two cubs feeding on a partially butchered, six-point bull elk. Ground crews found the hunters' bodies. This time, a mother bear evidently killed two hunters as they butchered their trophy elk.

In some ways, there's nothing new about bears eating hunters' scraps. Grizzly bears no doubt cleaned up the remains of woolly mammoths killed by hunters ten thousand years ago. Bears have simply adapted with the times. U.S. Fish and Wildlife Service biologist Wayne Kasworm says bears in Montana's Yaak Valley patrol hunters' favorite roads at night, cleaning up the remains of moose and white-tailed deer. Bears near Yellowstone National Park leave the sanctuary of the park during hunting season to cash in on elk offal in surrounding national forests.

The amount of protein hunters leave for scavengers is staggering. The Inter Agency Grizzly Bear Study Team estimated that hunters leave 370 tons of guts, hide, bones, and meat scraps on the land surrounding Yellowstone National Park. Most of that is elk. "A gut pile or carcass is like a huge pile of gold for a bear," said Jonkel. "It's like someone giving you free money right before winter so you can go buy ten cords of firewood. Grizzly bears have always followed wolves and cougars to their kills. It only makes sense that they would do the same with people where there is a lot of big-game hunting. It's a learned behavior, something mother bears pass on to their young."

Having bears eat gut piles isn't necessarily bad. The habit grows dangerous when a bear's desire for game meat overwhelms its normal caution around people. This may be compounded when bears eat trash, pet food, or other food left out at rural homes or camps and have learned to associate human scent with food.

• • •

MEANWHILE ON THE GAME RANGE, state and federal wildlife authorities knew there was at least one bear in the woods that had killed a hunter and been rewarded for it.

The Wednesday afternoon after the searchers found Hilston, Warden Campbell placed two culvert traps next to the elk carcass. Wednesday night, a bear visited the trap. The bear stuck its head inside, ate a bit of bait, and then climbed atop the trap. The commotion triggered the trap's door, without a bear inside.

On Thursday, a team of bear trappers from state and federal wildlife agencies in Missoula and Kalispell arrived at the scene. The trappers removed the culvert traps and set three spring-loaded cable foot snares made of quarter-inch aircraft steel. Trappers buried the snares in loose duff, anchored them to trees, and used chunks of the elk as bait. The trappers hauled off the excess elk carcass so that meat wouldn't be available. The snares had special radio transmitters so trappers could tell from a distance if the trap had been tripped.

Friday morning the radio signal indicated they might have a bear. Back at the trap site, they found not one bear, but three. A 380-pound female grizzly was in one snare, while a 100-pound cub was in another. A third cub, also about 100 pounds, was free and running between the two.

It turned out the female was wearing a radio collar. She had been caught before. In 1999 a bear had been killing stock at a ranch near the Blackfoot-Clearwater Game Range. Biologist caught this female but didn't believe she was the stock-killer. They outfitted her with a radio collar and released her in the game range. They followed her for a year and she lived a typical, uneventful life. In 2000 the batteries in her radio collar died. She gave no clue that she would ever cause trouble.

But now, according to the tracks on the ground and other circumstantial evidence, this bear had returned to the attack scene twice. Authorities decided these bears probably killed Hilston and thus should be destroyed. They shot the three bears and shipped the carcasses to a Bozeman laboratory for more tests, trying to make certain these bears killed Hilston. Weeks later, DNA testing proved inconclusive, but the bite marks on Hilston's body did match the dental signature of the female's teeth. Authorities felt reassured they had killed the bears that killed Hilston.

Hilston's death was a "very, very tragic event for all of us," Montana Department of Fish, Wildlife and Parks's spokesman Bill Thompson said. "We consider hunters and anglers to be part of our family and we feel the loss also."

* * *

GRIZZLY BEARS ARE NOTHING if not controversial. Wildlife officials knew they would catch flak for destroying the three bears. After all, Montana grizzlies are protected under the Endangered Species Act, and at the time there was no definitive proof that the three bears were the killers. Federal grizzly bear recovery coordinator Chris Servheen could see those criticisms coming. He told the local *Missoulian* newspaper destroying these bears was the best thing to do.

"We do not protect bears, we manage them. A bear that exhibits unnatural aggression is not good for the population," Servheen said. "The safety of people is primary here. We can't allow mother bears to teach their young to be aggressive to people."

Hilston's death renewed the call in some quarters to resume Montana's hunting season for grizzly bears. Montana grizzlies were listed as threatened under the Endangered Species Act in 1975. The state had a special exception to continue a limited bear hunt until 1991 when environmental and animal protection groups sued. A judge ruled the state didn't have the scientific basis to support a hunt and ended it. Jean Johnson, executive director of the Montana Outfitters and Guides Association, was among the first to call for resuming the bear hunt. She said a hunting season would restore a healthy fear in bears that had been protected for too long.

Hilston's brother-in-law, Tom Sidor, emphatically agrees. "We are absolutely not anti-grizzly. We believe there is a place for them in the world and a place for them in Montana," he said. "But where are we going to draw the line?"

Sidor is also concerned that an expanding grizzly population is putting more people in danger in places like the prairie near the Rocky Mountain Front and the Blackfoot-Clearwater Game Range, which are not widely considered modern grizzly habitat. Likewise, the Montana Department of Fish, Wildlife and Parks has argued for twenty-five years that hunting is necessary to keep bears fearful of humans.

Experts are divided on the subject. In his classic book *Bear Attacks, Their Causes and Avoidance,* Stephen Herrero doubts hunting makes bears significantly more wary. He wrote: "Hunting is in fact a poor way to teach a bear to do anything since there is little opportunity to learn. Death isn't an instructor—it's an eliminator."

While hunting may eliminate unusually bold bears, it cannot guarantee that an attack like that which killed Hilston will never happen. Grizzlies in British Columbia have always been hunted. That didn't prevent the fatal mauling of the two elk hunters in 1995.

Jonkel says hunters can improve their safety by hunting in pairs, by carrying pepper spray, and by learning to recognize and interpret bear sign. Most importantly, keep a clean camp and get meat out of the woods within twenty-four hours, if possible.

The risk of hunting in grizzly country can be mitigated but probably not entirely eliminated. Nor should it be. The lure of elk hunting is that it takes place in wild country where things happen that no one can predict. Even in elk country thick with bears, hunters are more likely to die from a falling tree, a chilling rainstorm, or a broken bone. For many of us who hunt in grizzly country every year, the great bear is part of the wildness that we seek.

Still, for the sake of people and bears alike, this conflict between bears and hunters is not being ignored. Hunters and wildlife managers are assessing the "dinnerbell bear" problem to determine the actual risk and think of creative ways to solve it. Shortly after Hilston's death, another hunter saw a grizzly and shot it, wounding it at close range. The bear took off running and was never seen again.

"People are kind of edgy right now," said Warden Jeff Campbell. "I see more people hunting in pairs, more people making sure to be back in their rigs before dark. Everyone is a little bit paranoid—maybe even a bit too much so."

Conclusion: One Last Mystery

Dr. Brian "Barney" Reeves walked along the barren bottom of a dry reservoir on the western edge of the Montana Great Plains. The Rocky Mountains rose majestically behind his back, but his eyes were fixed on the arid mud flats underfoot. Drought had dried the reservoir, offering Reeves a rare glimpse into the deep past.

Reeves, one of the foremost archaeologists of the Rocky Mountain Front, explained that this flat land was a long-term home of ancient hunters living thousands of years before Christ. We found flakes of obsidian, chips of spear points carried hundreds of miles to these hunting grounds. Cooking hearths—obscure rings of stone full of ash and bone—revealed themselves on the ground. Reeves pointed out bones of bighorn sheep and bison, the staple foods of these people. He explained that he had examined uncounted scores of these hearths and only once found a bear bone, the femur of a black bear. As far as he knew, grizzly bears were taboo food in prehistoric times, as they were to many tribes in historic times.

We crouched beside one of the hearths, examining the bones on the surface. We realized these were not bones—they were teeth. Teeth are harder than bone and last much longer, but these were splintered and almost disintegrated. These were pointed teeth, longer than a man's finger—the fangs of a giant predator. Grizzly teeth.

We counted eight of them and realized that thousands of years before, someone had stood in this spot and cooked the heads of at least two grizzly bears. Why? Was it simply practical, or something spiritual? Was it a meal? Or an elaborate ceremony? The mourning, or even vengeance, of some lost loved one? A celebration rite for the coming of spring? What story was told about these teeth? Certainly, there was one.

No one knows. No one can ever know. Modern people see the bear as a complex blend of myth and fact. I imagine the ancient ones saw bears in much the same way. We jotted notes, made a few photographs, and left the fragments on the ground to molder in their mystery.

· · ·

BEAR STORIES HAVE BEEN A PART of Montana long before there was a Montana. We have our own bear stories today, passed from friend to friend, family to family. The grizzly bear is our state animal, the mascot of our university football team. The same can be said for California, except that Montana still has its flesh-and-fur grizzly bears in the mountains, not just bear symbols on flags and pennants. Montanans have taken great steps to make sure that bears remain part of their custom and culture. Montana without its grizzly bears might still be called Montana, but it would be a far different, far lesser place.

It seemed to me that if these ancient humans who hunted bison and bighorns with spears on the Rocky Mountain Front could live alongside the grizzly, then so can we. With all of our computers, weaponry, and claims of intellectual superiority, we have no excuse for failure.

Grizzly bears are, in an often-misused word, awesome. More than other animals, grizzlies carry the wilderness on their backs. They are sometimes frightening, sometimes inconvenient, sometimes difficult, but they are always fascinating, always complicated. Hurrah for them. May they roam Montana forever.

Sources

Brown, Gary. *Great Bear Almanac.* 1993. The Lyons Press. New York.

Busch, H. Robert. *The Grizzly Almanac.* 2000. The Lyons Press. New York.

Craighead, John L., et al. *The Grizzly Bears of Yellowstone: Their Ecology in the Yellowstone Ecosystem, 1959-92.* 1995. Island Press. Washington, D. C.

Cutright, Paul R., *Lewis & Clark, Pioneering Naturalists.* 1969. University of Nebraska Press. Lincoln, Nebraska.

Frances, Fuller Victor. *The River of the West.* 1875. Reprinted 1974 by Brooks-Sterling Co. Oakland, California.

Gowans, Fred R. *Mountain Man and Grizzly.* 1986. Mountain Grizzly Press. Orem, Utah.

Hanna, Warren L. *The Grizzlies of Glacier.* 1978. Mountain Press Publishing Co. Missoula, Montana.

Herrero, Stephen. *Bear Attacks: Their Causes and Avoidance.* 1983. Lyons and Burford Press.

McMillion, Scott. *Mark of the Grizzly.* 1998. Falcon Press. Helena, Montana.

Mills, Enos A. *The Grizzly.* 1919. Comstock Editions, Inc. Sausalito, California.

Prodgers, Jeanette. *The Only Good Bear is a Dead Bear: A Collection of the West's Best Bear Stories*. 1986. Prodgers. Butte, Montana.

Russell, Andy. *Grizzly Country*. 1967. Knopf. New York.

Schullery, Paul. *The Bears of Yellowstone*. 1986. Robert Rinehart. Boulder, Colorado.

Shepherd, Paul and Sanders, Barry. *The Sacred Paw: The Bear in Nature, Myth and Literature*. 1985. Penguin Books. New York.

Shirley, Gayle C. *Four-legged Legends of Montana*. 1993. Falcon Press. Helena, Montana.

Whittlesey, Lee H. *Death In Yellowstone: Accidents and Foolhardiness in the First National Park*. 1995. Roberts Reinhart Press. Boulder, Colorado.

Yaak Valley Forest Council. *Archipelago: Notes From An Inland Island*. 2000. YVFC. Libby, Montana.

Bear Conservation Organizations

There are many people working hard to make certain that
grizzly and black bears remain a part of Montana's future. I
would like to highlight two non-profit groups that are always
in need of memberships and money. They are well known
for creative and constructive ways of resolving disputes
between people and bears. If you would like to help
Montana's bears, these are two good places to start:

The Wind River Bear Institute
P.O. Box 307
Heber City, UT 84032
www.beardogs.org

Carrie Hunt of WRBI has spearheaded the use of "bear
shepherding" or using highly trained Kerelian bear dogs to
teach bears to avoid rural homes, campgrounds and other
trouble spots.

Defenders of Wildlife
1244 19th St. N. W.
Washington D.C. 20036
www.defenders.org

Defenders helps reimburse ranchers for livestock killed by
grizzlies and wolves.

About the Author

BENJAMIN LONG is an outdoorsman, conservationist and author. His reporting and writing about the natural world has earned him several awards, including the Chinook Literary Prize. He is the author of *Backtracking: by foot, canoe and Subaru on the Lewis and Clark Trail,* and he writes for several newspapers and magazines, including *High Country News, Bugle, Montana Living, Montana,* and *Defenders.* He lives in Kalispell with his wife and enjoys spending as much time as possible in grizzly country.